OMMO AIR FRYER OVEN COOKBOOK

1000-DAY DELICIOUS RECIPES FOR BEGINNERS

PAUL BAYNES

CONTENTS

INTRODUCTION

How Does Air Frying Work?

Ever wonder why fried mozzarella sticks and potato chips get crunchy? All that hot oil causes the surface water in food to boil super-quick and exit as steam — leaving the outside of your food dry, which is the perfect setup for golden brown, crispy results.

Air fryers are full of hot air, literally. Air replaces oil in this machine and crisps and browns while it circulates around food. Air fried foods generally have less fat and calories per serving compared to their doppelganger fried version.

Seeing the Benefits of the OMMO Air Fryer Oven

1. Protect the food's nutrients

Unlike deep frying, Air Fryers do not deconstruct the food's good nutrients and add on bad fats. If you think your yasai tempura (deep-fried battered vegetables) are healthy, here is news for you; while they may look like they are full of nutritious elements, the deep frying process would have destroyed the beneficial vitamins and minerals contained in the vegetables.

2. Keeping cancer at bay

For some oils (e.g. olive and flax seed), their chemical structure changes in high heat causing them to transform into bad forms of fat. Additionally, since there is little oil used, there is little chance for food to produce carcinogens that activate cancer cells.

3. Calories are good, but too much spells trouble!

Fried foods are high in calories which is the leading cause of weight gain and obesity. Obesity will then lead to a plethora of killer diseases such as diabetes, cancer, stroke, sleep problems, and immobility to name a few. Adopting a low-fat diet will help you maintain your weight or prevent weight loss because essentially, you are eating fewer calories. Therefore, eating Air Fryer-cooked food will support your weight loss journey.

4. Build a fortress for your heart

Eating food fried with an Air Fryer reduces the risk of heart diseases and protects your body by helping you absorb the necessary nutrients. Since a minimal amount of oil is used to prepare food, you can be sure that your body will not accumulate excessive fats in the long run. Instead, the optimal amount of oil used will help your body protect your heart.

5. Keeping your kidneys clear

Consuming excess amounts of deep-fried food will impair your kidney's ability to filter our harmful fats. Therefore, eating food fried by an Air Fryer can help you lower your risks of getting kidney disease. If you are finding it difficult to quit deep-fried food cold turkey, using an Air Fryer will ease your transition to a healthier diet.

6. Reduce the worries of fat

Fat is a macro nutrient – it is essential to help control inflammation, blood clotting, maintaining healthy hair and skin, prevent heart diseases, provide energy and assist in the absorption of vitamins A, D, E, and K. While it is important to your bodily functions, too much of it is detrimental to health. An Air Fryer is a modern kitchen appliance that fries food using heated hot air by using at most a tablespoon of oil. This way, you are able to eat fried food without worrying about the negative effects of fatty food on your health.

Tricks on How to Use the Accessories of the OMMO Air Fryer Oven

1. Heating Element Protection Cover

The protection cover can prevent the food from contacting the heating element.

Let the side with wire handle face down, slide along the top plastic shelf near the heating element in the oven to install the protection cover. Take out the protection cover by pulling the wire handle.

2. Air Flow Racks

The air flow racks can be used not only for dehydration but also to cook crispy snacks or reheat foods like pizza.

Slide along the rack shelf to install or take out the air flow racks.

3. Rotisserie Fork Set

The rotisserie fork set is used for roasting large meat or whole chicken.

Install a fork backwards to the gear on the shaft. Force shaft lengthwise through meat/chicken in center. Install another fork towards the meat/chicken. Slide both forks into meat/chicken and adjust the meat/chicken to the middle of the shaft, then drive the screws to lock the forks in position.

You can adjust the forks closer to the middle if needed but never outwards to the groove of both ends.

To install the rotisserie fork set, let the end with the gear face towards left, insert the grooves on both ends of the shaft into the rotating shelf.

4. Rotisserie Basket

Great for fries, roasting nuts and other snacks.

Use the hasp to open and lock the rotisserie basket. To install the rotisserie basket, let the the gear face towards left, insert the grooves on both ends of the shaft into the rotating shelf.

5. Fetch Tool

Used to remove the rotisserie basket or fork set from the appliance.

Place the fetch tool under the shaft at both side of the rotisserie basket or fork set, then gently extract the rotisserie basket or fork set out.

6. Drip Tray

Cook with the drip tray for easy clean ups.

Put the drip tray into the bottom of the appliance when in use. It is easy to take out for cleaning.

7. Door

The door is detachable for easy cleaning.

Open the door at a 30°angle from the appliance and gently put on or take off the door.

The appliance will not work with the door open

- To keep your air fryer oven in good working order, make sure to remove all food residues and grease splatters from interior surfaces on a regular basis. Regular cleaning will also reduce the fire hazard risk.

- Unplug the air fryer oven from the power supply. Allow the appliance to cool.
- Remove all accessories (crumb tray, oven rack, food tray, air-frying basket, pizza pan) from the oven cavity.

Interior walls and oven door

- Use a damp cloth and mild detergent solution on a sponge to clean the interior walls and door of the air fryer oven. Repeat with a dry, clean cloth.
- Never use harsh abrasives, corrosive products or as these could damage the oven surface. Never use steel wool pads or other abrasive cleaning products. Abrasive cleaners, scrubbing brushes and chemical cleaners will damage the coating on this unit. Pieces can break off the and touch electrical parts involving a risk of electrical shock.
- If scrubbing is necessary, use a nonabrasive nylon or polyester mesh pad.

Crumb tray

- To remove crumbs and drippings from the bottom of the oven, slide out the crumb tray and discard any crumbs. Wipe the crumb tray clean and replace. To remove baked-on grease, soak the tray in hot, sudsy water or use nonabrasive cleaners. Never operate the oven without the crumb tray in place!

Exterior surfaces

- Wipe the appliance housing clean with a damp cloth and a mild detergent. Apply the cleansing agent to the cloth, not directly onto the oven. Dry thoroughly

BREAKFAST

English Muffin Express Sandwich

Servings: 2

Cooking Time: 5 Minutes

Ingredients:

- 1 tablespoon mayonnaise
- 1 tablespoon chopped green onions, white and green portions
- ¼ teaspoon garlic powder
- 1 tablespoon unsalted butter, plus softened butter for spreading
- 2 large eggs
- Kosher salt and freshly ground black pepper
- 2 English muffins, split
- 2 slices Canadian bacon or thin, deli-style cooked ham
- 2 slices cheddar cheese

Directions:

1. Stir the mayonnaise, green onions, and garlic powder in a small bowl; set aside.
2. Melt 1 tablespoon butter in a small, nonstick skillet over medium heat. Whisk 1 egg in a small bowl and season with salt and pepper. Pour the egg into the skillet. Cook about 1 minute or until the egg is cooked on the bottom, gently turn the egg, and cook the second side. Remove the cooked egg from the skillet and keep warm. Repeat with the second egg.
3. Toast the English muffins in the toaster oven. Remove the toasted muffins and lightly spread the softened butter on the cut surface of each muffin. Place a slice of Canadian bacon and cheese on the bottom piece of each muffin. (Fold the cheese as necessary and do not allow the edges of the cheese to hang over the edges of the muffin.) Place the muffin, cheese-side up, in a baking pan. Heat on Toast or Broil for 1 to 2 minutes or until the cheese is melted.
4. Spread the top piece of each English muffin with the mayonnaise mixture.
5. Remove the cheese-topped English muffin from the toaster oven. Place the cooked egg on top of the melted cheese, folding to fit, as necessary. Top with the other piece of the English muffin, mayonnaise side down. Serve warm.

Southern-style Biscuits

Servings: 10

Cooking Time: 12 Minutes

Ingredients:

- 2 cups all-purpose flour
- 1 tablespoon baking powder
- 1 teaspoon table salt
- 4 tablespoons cold, unsalted butter, cut into bits
- ¾ to 1 cup buttermilk

Directions:

1. Preheat the toaster oven to 450 °F.
2. Combine the flour, baking powder, and salt in a large bowl. Using a pastry cutter or two knives, cut the butter into the flour mixture until the mixture is crumbly throughout. Pour in the buttermilk and gently mix until just combined.
3. Turn the dough onto a lightly floured surface and knead lightly about 8 times. Roll the dough, using a rolling pin, until about ½ inch thick. Cut out rounds using a 2 ½ -inch cutter. Place on an ungreased 12 x 12-inch baking pan or 8-inch round pan.
4. Bake for 10 to 12 minutes or until golden brown. Let cool slightly before serving warm.

Roasted Tomato And Cheddar Rolls

Servings: 12
Cooking Time: 55 Minutes

Ingredients:

- 4 Roma tomatoes
- ½ clove garlic, minced
- 1 tablespoon olive oil
- ¼ teaspoon dried thyme
- salt and freshly ground black pepper
- 4 cups all-purpose flour
- 1 teaspoon active dry yeast
- 2 teaspoons sugar
- 2 teaspoons salt
- 1 tablespoon olive oil
- 1 cup grated Cheddar cheese, plus more for sprinkling at the end
- 1½ cups water

Directions:

1. Cut the Roma tomatoes in half, remove the seeds with your fingers and transfer to a bowl. Add the garlic, olive oil, dried thyme, salt and freshly ground black pepper and toss well.
2. Preheat the toaster oven to 390°F.
3. Place the tomatoes, cut side up in the air fryer oven and air-fry for 10 minutes. The tomatoes should just start to brown. Redistribute the tomatoes, and air-fry for another 5 to 10 minutes at 330°F until the tomatoes are no longer juicy. Let the tomatoes cool and then rough chop them.
4. Combine the flour, yeast, sugar and salt in the bowl of a stand mixer. Add the olive oil, chopped roasted tomatoes and Cheddar cheese to the flour mixture and start to mix using the dough hook attachment. As you're mixing, add 1¼ cups of the water, mixing until the dough comes together. Continue to knead the dough with the dough hook for another 10 minutes, adding enough water to the dough to get it to the right consistency.
5. Transfer the dough to an oiled bowl, cover with a clean kitchen towel and let it rest and rise until it has doubled in volume – about 1 to 2 hours. Then, divide the dough into 12 equal portions. Roll each portion of dough into a ball. Lightly coat each dough ball with oil and let the dough balls rest and rise a second time, covered lightly with plastic wrap for 45 minutes. (Alternately, you can place the rolls in the refrigerator overnight and take them out 2 hours before you bake them.)
6. Preheat the toaster oven to 360°F.
7. Spray the dough balls and the air fryer oven with a little olive oil. Place three rolls at a time in the air fryer oven and bake for 10 minutes. Add a little grated Cheddar cheese on top of the rolls for the last 2 minutes of air frying for an attractive finish.

Savory Breakfast Bread Pudding

Servings: 4

Cooking Time: 30 Minutes

Ingredients:

- Oil spray (hand-pumped)
- 4 slices whole-wheat bread, cubed
- 1 cup frozen potato hash browns, thawed
- 5 large eggs
- 1 cup whole milk
- ½ cup diced ham
- ½ cup shredded cheddar cheese
- 1 teaspoon fresh parsley, chopped
- ⅛ teaspoon sea salt
- ⅛ teaspoon freshly ground black pepper

Directions:

1. Place the baking tray on position 1 and preheat the toaster oven on BAKE to 350°F for 5 minutes.
2. Lightly oil an 8-inch-square baking dish with spray.
3. Spread the bread cubes and potatoes in the baking dish evenly.
4. In a medium bowl, combine the eggs, milk, ham, cheese, parsley, salt, and pepper.
5. Pour the egg mixture over the bread and potatoes in the dish.
6. Bake for 30 minutes. The bread pudding should be lightly golden, the eggs set, and a knife inserted in the center should come out clean.
7. Cool the pudding for 5 minutes and serve.

Hot Italian-style Sub

Servings:3

Cooking Time: 15 Minutes

Ingredients:

- 3 Italian-style hoagie rolls
- 3 tablespoons unsalted butter, softened
- 1 teaspoon Italian seasoning
- ½ teaspoon garlic powder
- 9 slices salami
- 12 slices pepperoni
- 3 thin slices ham
- 3 tablespoons giardiniera mix, chopped
- 6 tablespoons shredded mozzarella cheese

Directions:

1. Preheat the toaster oven to 350°F. Split the rolls lengthwise, cutting almost but not quite though the roll. Place the sandwiches in a 12 x 12-inch baking pan, side by side with the open side face up.
2. Combine the butter, Italian seasoning, and garlic powder in a small bowl. Spread evenly on the inside of the hoagie rolls.
3. Layer a third of the salami, pepperoni, and ham on each sandwich. Sprinkle with the giardiniera mix and mozzarella cheese.
4. Bake for 10 to 15 minutes or until heated through and the cheese is melted.

Crispy Bacon

Servings: 6

Cooking Time: 20 Minutes

Ingredients:

- 12 ounces bacon

Directions:

1. Preheat the toaster oven to 350°F for 3 minutes.
2. Lay out the bacon in a single layer, slightly overlapping the strips of bacon.
3. Air fry for 10 minutes or until desired crispness.
4. Repeat until all the bacon has been cooked.

Tuna Tarragon Picnic Loaf

Servings: 4

Cooking Time: 10 Minutes

Ingredients:

- 1 French baguette, sliced in half lengthwise, then quartered
- Filling:
- 1 6-ounce can tuna in water, well drained
- 2 tablespoons chopped onion
- 2 tablespoons chopped Spanish olives with pimientos, drained
- 2 tablespoons chopped fresh parsley
- 2 tablespoons chopped bell pepper
- 1 teaspoon dried tarragon
- Salt and butcher's pepper to taste
- ½ cup shredded low-fat mozzarella cheese

Directions:

1. Remove enough bread from each quarter to make a small cavity for the sandwich filling.
2. Combine all the filling ingredients and spoon the mixture in equal portions into each of the bread quarter cavities. Sprinkle each quarter with equal portions of mozzarella cheese.
3. BROIL on a broiling rack with a pan underneath for 10 minutes, or until the bread is lightly browned and the cheese is melted. If your toaster oven cannot accommodate 4 French bread quarters, broil them in two batches. Slice and serve.

Huevos Rancheros

Servings: 2

Cooking Time: 60 Minutes

Ingredients:

- 1 (28-ounce) can diced tomatoes
- 1½ teaspoons packed brown sugar
- 1½ teaspoons lime juice
- 1 small onion, chopped
- ¼ cup canned chopped green chiles
- 2 tablespoons extra-virgin olive oil
- 1½ tablespoons chili powder
- 2 garlic cloves, sliced thin
- ¼ teaspoon plus ⅛ teaspoon table salt, divided
- 2 ounces pepper Jack cheese, shredded (½ cup)
- 4 large eggs
- ⅛ teaspoon pepper
- ½ avocado, halved, pitted, and diced
- 2 tablespoons minced fresh cilantro
- 2 scallions, sliced thin
- 4 (6-inch) corn tortillas, warmed

Directions:

1. Adjust toaster oven rack to middle position and preheat the toaster oven to 450 degrees. Drain tomatoes in fine-mesh strainer set over bowl, pressing with rubber spatula to extract as much juice as possible. Combine ¾ cup drained tomato juice, sugar, and lime juice in bowl; set aside. Discard remaining drained juice.
2. Combine tomatoes, onion, chiles, oil, chili powder, garlic, and ¼ teaspoon salt in bowl, then spread mixture evenly on small rimmed baking sheet. Roast until charred in spots, 25 to 30 minutes, stirring and redistributing mixture into even layer halfway through roasting.
3. Remove sheet from oven. Carefully stir reserved tomato juice mixture into roasted vegetables, season with salt and pepper to taste, and spread into even layer. Sprinkle pepper Jack over top and, using back of spoon, make 4 evenly spaced indentations in cheese, each about 3 inches in diameter. Crack 1 egg into each hole and sprinkle with remaining ⅛ teaspoon salt and pepper.
4. Roast until whites are just beginning to set but still have some movement when sheet is shaken, 7 to 8 minutes for runny yolks or 9 to 10 minutes for soft but set yolks. Top with avocado, cilantro, and scallions. Serve immediately with tortillas.

Savory Salsa Cheese Rounds

Servings: 6

Cooking Time: 6 Minutes

Ingredients:

- 1 French baguette, cut to make 12
- 1-inch slices (rounds)
- ¼ cup olive oil
- 1 cup Tomato Salsa (recipe follows)
- ½ cup shredded low-fat mozzarella
- 2 tablespoons finely chopped fresh cilantro

Directions:

1. Brush both sides of each round with olive oil.
2. Spread one side of each slice with salsa and sprinkle each with mozzarella. Place the rounds in an oiled or nonstick 8½ × 8½ × 2-inch square baking (cake) pan.
3. BROIL for 6 minutes, or until the cheese is melted and the rounds are lightly browned. Garnish with the chopped cilantro and serve.

Baked Parmesan Eggs

Servings: 4

Cooking Time: 10 Minutes

Ingredients:

- 4 large eggs, each cracked into a small 1-cup baking dish
- 4 tablespoons grated Parmesan cheese
- 4 tablespoons fat-free half-and-half
- Salt and freshly ground black pepper

Directions:

1. Preheat the toaster oven to 400° F.
2. Top each egg with 1 tablespoon Parmesan cheese and 1 tablespoon half-and-half. Season to taste with salt and pepper and add any preferred additions.
3. BAKE for 10 minutes, or to your preference, testing the eggs by touching the surface with a spoon for the desired firmness after 5 minutes.

French Toast Casserole

Servings: 6

Cooking Time: 60 Minutes

Ingredients:

- 1 tablespoon unsalted butter, softened, plus 6 tablespoons unsalted butter, melted, divided
- ¾ cup packed (5¼ ounces) brown sugar
- 1 tablespoon ground cinnamon
- ½ teaspoon ground nutmeg
- ⅛ teaspoon table salt
- 18 slices potato sandwich bread, divided
- 2½ cups whole milk
- 6 large eggs
- ¼ cup sliced almonds, toasted
- Confectioners' sugar

Directions:

1. Adjust toaster oven rack to middle position and preheat the toaster oven to 350 degrees. Grease 13 by 9-inch baking dish with softened butter. Mix brown sugar, cinnamon, nutmeg, and salt together in bowl.
2. Sprinkle 3 tablespoons brown sugar mixture evenly over bottom of prepared dish. Place 6 bread slices (use bread heels here) in even layer in bottom of dish. Brush bread with 1½ tablespoons melted butter and sprinkle with 3 tablespoons sugar mixture.
3. Place 6 bread slices in single layer over first layer, brush with 1½ tablespoons melted butter, then sprinkle with 3 tablespoons sugar mixture. Place remaining 6 bread slices over previous layer and brush with 1½ tablespoons melted butter.
4. In separate bowl, whisk milk and eggs until well combined, then pour evenly over bread. Gently press down on layers with spatula to saturate bread. (Casserole can be covered and refrigerated for up to 12 hours.)
5. Sprinkle with almonds and remaining sugar mixture. Bake until casserole is slightly puffed and golden brown and bubbling around edges, 30 to 35 minutes, rotating dish halfway through baking. Transfer dish to wire rack, brush with remaining 1½ tablespoons melted butter, and let cool for 15 minutes. Sprinkle with confectioners' sugar and serve.

Strawberry Shortcake With Buttermilk Biscuits

Servings: 8

Cooking Time: 15 Minutes

Ingredients:

- 1 quart fresh strawberries, rinsed and sliced
- 2 tablespoons sugar
- 1 tablespoon lemon juice
- Buttermilk biscuit mix:
- 2 cups unbleached flour
- 2 teaspoons baking powder
- ½ teaspoon baking soda
- Salt to taste
- ¼ cup margarine
- 1 cup low-fat buttermilk
- Vegetable oil
- Nonfat whipped topping

Directions:

1. Preheat the toaster oven to 400° F.
2. Combine the strawberries, sugar, and lemon juice in a large bowl, mixing well to blend. Set aside.
3. Combine the flour, baking powder, baking soda, and salt in a large bowl. Add the margarine, cutting it into the flour with a knife or pastry cutter. Add just enough buttermilk so that the dough will hold together when pinched.
4. Turn the dough out onto a lightly floured surface and knead 5 or 6 times. Drop the dough from a tablespoon onto an oiled or nonstick 6½ × 10-inch baking sheet. Make 8 mounds 1½ inches across and flatten the tops with a spoon.
5. BAKE for 15 minutes, or until the biscuits are lightly browned. Cool. Spoon on the fresh strawberries. Top with nonfat whipped topping and serve.

Tuscan Toast

Servings: 4

Cooking Time: 5 Minutes

Ingredients:

- ¼ cup butter
- ½ teaspoon lemon juice
- ½ clove garlic
- ½ teaspoon dried parsley flakes
- 4 slices Italian bread, 1-inch thick

Directions:

1. Place butter, lemon juice, garlic, and parsley in a food processor. Process about 1 minute, or until garlic is pulverized and ingredients are well blended.
2. Spread garlic butter on both sides of bread slices.
3. Place bread slices upright in air fryer oven. (They can lie flat but cook better standing on end.)
4. Air-fry at 390°F for 5minutes or until toasty brown.

LUNCH AND DINNER

Easy Oven Lasagne

Servings: 4

Cooking Time: 60 Minutes

Ingredients:

- 6 uncooked lasagna noodles, broken in half
- 1 15-ounce jar marinara sauce
- ½ pound ground turkey or chicken breast
- ½ cup part-skim ricotta cheese
- ½ cup shredded part-skim mozzarella cheese
- 2 tablespoons chopped fresh oregano leaves or 1 teaspoon dried oregano
- 2 tablespoons chopped fresh basil leaves or 1 teaspoon dried basil
- 1 tablespoon garlic cloves, minced
- ¼ cup grated Parmesan cheese
- Salt and freshly ground black pepper to taste

Directions:

1. Preheat the toaster oven to 375° F.
2. Layer in a 1-quart 8½ × 8½ × 4-inch ovenproof baking dish in this order: 6 lasagna noodle halves, ½ jar of the marinara sauce, ½ cup water, half of the ground meat, half of the ricotta and mozzarella cheeses, half of the oregano and basil leaves, and half of the minced garlic. Repeat the layer, starting with the noodles. Cover the dish with aluminum foil.
3. BAKE, covered, for 50 minutes, or until the noodles are tender. Uncover, sprinkle the top with Parmesan cheese and bake for another 10 minutes, or until the liquid is reduced and the top is browned.

Yeast Dough For Two Pizzas

Servings: 8

Cooking Time: 20 Minutes

Ingredients:

- ¼ cup tepid water
- 1 cup tepid skim milk
- ½ teaspoon sugar
- 1 1¼-ounce envelope dry yeast
- 2 cups unbleached flour
- 1 tablespoon olive oil

Directions:

1. Preheat the toaster oven to 400° F.
2. Combine the water, milk, and sugar in a bowl. Add the yeast and set aside for 3 to 5 minutes, or until the yeast is dissolved.
3. Stir in the flour gradually, adding just enough to form a ball of the dough.
4. KNEAD on a floured surface until the dough is satiny, and then put the dough in a bowl in a warm place with a damp towel over the top. In 1 hour or when the dough has doubled in bulk, punch it down and divide it in half. Flatten the dough and spread it out to the desired thickness on an oiled or nonstick 9¾-inch-diameter pie pan. Spread with Homemade Pizza Sauce (recipe follows) and add any desired toppings.
5. BAKE for 20 minutes, or until the topping ingredients are cooked and the cheese is melted.

Spanish Rice

Servings: 4

Cooking Time: 45 Minutes

Ingredients:

- ¾ cup rice
- 2 tablespoons dry white wine
- 3 tablespoons olive oil
- 1 15-ounce can whole tomatoes
- ¼ cup thinly sliced onions
- 3 tablespoons chopped fresh cilantro
- 4 ½ cup chopped bell pepper
- 5 2 bay leaves
- Salt and a pinch of red pepper flakes to taste

Directions:

1. Preheat the toaster oven to 375° F.
2. Combine all the ingredients with 1 cup water in a 1-quart 8½ × 8½ × 4-inch ovenproof baking dish and adjust the seasonings. Cover with aluminum foil.
3. BAKE, covered, for 45 minutes, or until the rice is cooked, removing the cover after 30 minutes.

Very Quick Pizza

Servings: 1

Cooking Time: 3 Minutes

Ingredients:

- 2 tablespoons salsa
- 1 6-inch whole wheat pita bread
- 2 tablespoons shredded part-skim, low-moisture mozzarella cheese

Directions:

1. Spread the salsa on the pita bread and sprinkle with the cheese.
2. TOAST once, or until the cheese is melted.

Creamy Roasted Pepper Basil Soup

Servings: 4

Cooking Time: 35 Minutes

Ingredients:

- 1 5-ounce jar roasted peppers, drained ½ cup fresh basil leaves
- 1 cup fat-free half-and-half
- 1 cup skim milk
- 2 tablespoons reduced-fat cream cheese
- 1 teaspoon garlic powder
- 1 teaspoon paprika
- Salt and freshly ground black pepper to taste
- 2 tablespoons chopped fresh basil leaves (garnish for cold soup)
- 2 tablespoons grated Parmesan cheese (topping for hot soup)

Directions:

1. Preheat the toaster oven to 400° F.
2. Process all the ingredients in a blender or food processor until smooth. Transfer the mixture to a 1-quart 8½ × 8½ × 4-inch ovenproof baking dish.
3. BAKE, covered, for 35 minutes. Ladle into individual soup bowls and serve.

Oven-baked Couscous

Servings: 4

Cooking Time: 10 Minutes

Ingredients:

- 1 10-ounce package couscous
- 2 tablespoons olive oil
- 2 tablespoons canned chickpeas
- 2 tablespoons canned or frozen green peas
- 1 tablespoon chopped fresh parsley
- 3 scallions, chopped
- Salt and pepper to taste

Directions:

1. Preheat the toaster oven to 400° F.
2. Mix together all the ingredients with 2 cups water in a 1-quart 8½ × 8½ × 4-inch ovenproof baking dish. Adjust the seasonings to taste. Cover with aluminum foil.
3. BAKE, covered, for 10 minutes, or until the couscous and vegetables are tender. Adjust the seasonings to taste and fluff with a fork before serving.

Fresh Herb Veggie Pizza

Servings: 4

Cooking Time: 25 Minutes

Ingredients:

- 1 9-inch ready-made pizza crust
- 1 tablespoon olive oil
- 1 4-ounce can tomato paste
- 2 tablespoons shredded part-skim mozzarella
- 2 tablespoons grated Parmesan cheese
- 2 tablespoons crumbled feta cheese
- ½ bell pepper, chopped
- 1 tablespoon chopped fresh parsley
- 1 tablespoon chopped fresh oregano
- 1 tablespoon chopped fresh basil
- ½ teaspoon red pepper flakes
- Salt and freshly ground black pepper to taste
- Pizza mixture:
- 2 garlic cloves, minced
- 1 plum tomato, chopped

Directions:

1. Preheat the toaster oven to 400° F.
2. Brush the pizza crust with olive oil and spread the tomato paste evenly to cover.
3. Combine the ingredients for the pizza mixture and spread evenly on top of the tomato paste layer. Sprinkle the cheeses over all and season to taste. Place the pizza on the toaster oven rack.
4. BAKE for 25 minutes, or until the vegetables are cooked and the cheese is melted.

Oven-baked Rice

Servings: 2

Cooking Time: 40 Minutes

Ingredients:

- ¼ cup regular rice (not parboiled or precooked)
- Seasonings:
- 1 tablespoon olive oil
- 1 teaspoon dried parsley or
- 1 tablespoon chopped fresh parsley
- 1 teaspoon garlic powder or roasted garlic
- Salt and freshly ground black pepper to taste

Directions:

1. Preheat the toaster oven to 400° F.
2. Combine ¼ cups water and the rice in a 1-quart 8½ × 8½ × 4-inch ovenproof baking dish. Stir well to blend. Cover with aluminum foil.
3. BAKE, covered, for 30 minutes, or until the rice is almost cooked. Add the seasonings, fluff with a fork to combine the seasonings well, then let the rice sit, covered, for 10 minutes. Fluff once more before serving.

Honey Bourbon–glazed Pork Chops With Sweet Potatoes + Apples

Servings: 2

Cooking Time: 42 Minutes

Ingredients:

- Nonstick cooking spray
- 2 medium sweet potatoes, peeled and quartered
- 2 tablespoons bourbon
- 2 tablespoons honey
- 1 tablespoon canola or vegetable oil
- ½ teaspoon onion powder
- ½ teaspoon dry mustard
- ¼ teaspoon dried thyme leaves
- Kosher salt and freshly ground black pepper
- 2 bone-in pork chops, cut about ¾ inch thick
- 1 Granny Smith apple, not peeled, cored and cut into ½-inch wedges

Directions:

1. Preheat the toaster oven to 375°F. Spray a 12 x 12-inch baking pan with nonstick cooking spray.
2. Place the sweet potatoes on one side of the prepared pan. Spray with nonstick cooking spray. Bake, uncovered, for 20 minutes.
3. Meanwhile, stir the bourbon, honey, oil, onion powder, mustard, and thyme in a small bowl. Season with salt and pepper and set aside.
4. Turn the potatoes over. Place the pork chops on the other end of the pan in a single layer. Arrange the apple wedges around the potatoes and pork chops, stacking the apples as needed. Brush the bourbon mixture generously over all. Bake for 15 to 18 minutes or until the pork is done as desired and a meat thermometer registers a minimum of 145°F.
5. For additional browning, set the toaster oven to Broil and broil for 2 to 4 minutes, or until the edges are brown as desired.
6. Transfer to a serving platter. Spoon any drippings over the meat and vegetables. Let stand for 5 minutes before serving.

Pea Soup

Servings: 6

Cooking Time: 55 Minutes

Ingredients:

- 1 cup dried split peas, ground in a blender to a powderlike consistency
- 3 strips lean turkey bacon, uncooked and chopped
- ¼ cup grated carrots
- ¼ cup grated celery
- 2 tablespoons grated onion
- ½ teaspoon garlic powder
- Salt and freshly ground black pepper to taste
- Garnish:
- 2 tablespoons chopped fresh chives

Directions:

1. Preheat the toaster oven to 400° F.
2. Combine all the ingredients in a 1-quart 8½ × 8½ × 4-inch ovenproof baking dish, mixing well. Adjust the seasonings.
3. BAKE, covered, for 35 minutes. Remove from the oven and stir.
4. BAKE, covered, for another 20 minutes, or until the soup is thickened. Ladle the soup into individual soup bowls and garnish each with chopped fresh chives.

Individual Baked Eggplant Parmesan

Servings: 5

Cooking Time: 55 Minutes

Ingredients:

- 1 medium eggplant, cut into 1/2-inch thick slices
- 1 1/2 teaspoons salt
- 1 cup Slow Cooker Marinara Sauce
- 1 package (8 oz.) fresh mozzarella, cut into 8 slices, divided
- 1 package (0.75 oz.) fresh basil, leaves only, divided
- 1/4 cup grated Parmesan cheese, divided

Directions:

1. Sprinkle eggplant with salt and place in a colander to drain for 1 hour.
2. Preheat the toaster oven to 375°F. Spray baking pan and 5 (4-inch) ramekins with nonstick cooking spray.
3. Rinse eggplant thoroughly with water to remove salt. Press each slice between paper towels to remove extra water and salt. Place on papertowels to dry. Arrange a single layer of eggplant slices in baking pan.
4. Bake 25 to 30 minutes or until eggplant is tender. Remove slices to cooking rack. Repeat baking remaining eggplant. Reduce oven temperature to 350°F.
5. In each ramekin, layer 1 slice eggplant, 1 tablespoon sauce, 1 slice mozzarella, 1 basil leaf, 1 additional tablespoon sauce and sprinkle with Parmesan cheese. Repeat layers ending with a sprinkle of Parmesan cheese.
6. Bake 20 to 25 minutes or until cheese is melted and eggplant layers are heated through.

Favorite Baked Ziti

Servings: 4

Cooking Time: 30 Minutes

Ingredients:

- 2 tablespoons olive oil
- 1 small onion, diced
- 3 cloves garlic, minced
- ¼ teaspoon red pepper flakes
- 1 pound lean ground beef
- ½ teaspoon kosher salt
- ¼ cup dry red wine
- 1 (14.5-ounce) can crushed tomatoes
- 1 tablespoon tomato paste
- 16 ounces ziti, uncooked
- Nonstick cooking spray
- ⅓ cup grated Parmesan cheese
- 1 ½ cups shredded mozzarella cheese
- 2 ounces fresh mozzarella cheese, cut into cubes (about ½ cup)

Directions:

1. Heat the olive oil in a large skillet over medium-high heat. Add the onion and cook, stirring frequently, until tender, 3 to 4 minutes. Stir in the garlic and red pepper flakes. Add the ground beef and salt. Cook, breaking up the ground beef, until the meat is brown and cooked through. Drain well, if needed, and return to the skillet.
2. Add the wine and cook for 2 minutes. Add the tomatoes, tomato paste, and ¾ cup water. Reduce the heat and simmer, uncovered, for 20 to 25 minutes, stirring occasionally.
3. Cook the ziti according to the package directions, except reduce the cooking time to 7 minutes. The ziti will be harder than Al Dente, which is what you want. Drain and rinse under cold water. Transfer to a large bowl.
4. Preheat the toaster oven to 425 °F. Spray an 11 x 7 x 2 ½-inch baking dish with nonstick cooking spray. Spoon about 1 cup of the meat sauce into the prepared dish. Add half of the ziti in an even layer. Spoon about half of the remaining sauce over the ziti. Sprinkle with half the Parmesan and all the shredded mozzarella. Add the remaining half of ziti and cover with the remaining sauce. Sprinkle the remaining Parmesan on top.
5. Bake, covered, for 20 minutes. Remove from the oven and add the cubes of fresh mozzarella. Bake, uncovered, for an additional 10 minutes. If desired, turn to broil for a few minutes to make the top crispy and brown.
6. Remove from the oven and let stand for 10 minutes before serving.

Healthy Southwest Stuffed Peppers

Servings: 6

Cooking Time: 30 Minutes

Ingredients:

- 1 tablespoon oil
- 1 small onion, chopped
- 1 garlic clove, minced
- 1/2 pound ground turkey
- 1/2 cup drained black beans
- 1/2 cup whole kernel corn
- 1 jar (16 oz.) medium salsa, divided
- 1/2 cup cooked white rice
- 1/2 teaspoon chili powder
- 1/2 teaspoon salt
- 1/4 teaspoon ground cumin
- 1/4 teaspoon black pepper
- 3 medium peppers, halved lengthwise leaving stem on, seeded
- 1/3 cup shredded Monterey Jack cheese, divided
- Sour cream
- Chopped fresh cilantro

Directions:

1. Preheat the toaster oven to 350°F. Spray baking pan with nonstick cooking spray.
2. In a large skillet over medium-high, heat oil. Add onion and garlic, cook for 2 to 3 minutes.
3. Add turkey to skillet, cook, stirring frequently, for 6 to 8 minutes or until turkey is cooked through.
4. Stir black beans, corn, 1/2 cup salsa, rice, chili powder, salt, cumin and pepper into turkey mixture.
5. Fill each pepper half with turkey mixture, dividing mixture evenly among peppers.
6. Top each pepper half with remaining salsa.
7. Bake 20 minutes. Sprinkle with cheese and bake an additional 10 minutes or until heated through.
8. Top with sour cream and cilantro.

SNACKS APPETIZERS AND SIDES

Grilled Ham & Muenster Cheese On Raisin Bread

Servings: 1

Cooking Time: 10 Minutes

Ingredients:

- 2 slices raisin bread
- 2 tablespoons butter, softened
- 2 teaspoons honey mustard
- 3 slices thinly sliced honey ham (about 3 ounces)
- 4 slices Muenster cheese (about 3 ounces)
- 2 toothpicks

Directions:

1. Preheat the toaster oven to 370°F.
2. Spread the softened butter on one side of both slices of raisin bread and place the bread, buttered side down on the counter. Spread the honey mustard on the other side of each slice of bread. Layer 2 slices of cheese, the ham and the remaining 2 slices of cheese on one slice of bread and top with the other slice of bread. Remember to leave the buttered side of the bread on the outside.
3. Transfer the sandwich to the air fryer oven and secure the sandwich with toothpicks.
4. Air-fry at 370°F for 5 minutes. Flip the sandwich over, remove the toothpicks and air-fry for another 5 minutes. Cut the sandwich in half and enjoy!!

Loaded Potato Skins

Servings: 8

Cooking Time: 8 Minutes

Ingredients:

- 12 round baby potatoes
- 3 ounces cream cheese
- 4 slices cooked bacon, crumbled or chopped
- 2 green onions, finely chopped
- ½ cup grated cheddar cheese, divided
- ¼ cup sour cream
- 1 tablespoon milk
- 2 teaspoons hot sauce

Directions:

1. Preheat the toaster oven to 320°F.
2. Poke holes into the baby potatoes with a fork. Place the potatoes onto a microwave-safe plate and microwave on high for 4 to 5 minutes, or until soft to squeeze. Let the potatoes cool until they're safe to handle, about 5 minutes.
3. Meanwhile, in a medium bowl, mix together the cream cheese, bacon, green onions, and ¼ cup of the cheddar cheese; set aside.
4. Slice the baby potatoes in half. Using a spoon, scoop out the pulp, leaving enough pulp on the inside to retain the shape of the potato half. Place the potato pulp into the cream cheese mixture and mash together with a fork. Using a spoon, refill the potato halves with filling.
5. Place the potato halves into the air fryer oven and top with the remaining ¼ cup of cheddar cheese.
6. Cook the loaded baked potato bites in batches for 8 minutes.
7. Meanwhile, make the sour cream sauce. In a small bowl, whisk together the sour cream, milk, and hot sauce. Add more hot sauce if desired.
8. When the potatoes have all finished cooking, place them onto a serving platter and serve with sour cream sauce drizzled over the top or as a dip.

Turkey Bacon Dates

Servings: 16

Cooking Time: 7 Minutes

Ingredients:

- 16 whole, pitted dates
- 16 whole almonds
- 6 to 8 strips turkey bacon

Directions:

1. Stuff each date with a whole almond.
2. Depending on the size of your stuffed dates, cut bacon strips into halves or thirds. Each strip should be long enough to wrap completely around a date.
3. Wrap each date in a strip of bacon with ends overlapping and secure with toothpicks.
4. Place in air fryer oven and air-fry at 390°F for 7 minutes, until bacon is as crispy as you like.
5. Drain on paper towels or wire rack. Serve hot or at room temperature.

Mozzarella-stuffed Arancini

Servings: 14

Cooking Time: 20 Minutes

Ingredients:

- Pie Crust
- 3½ cups low sodium chicken stock
- 4 tablespoons unsalted butter, divided
- 1 medium onion, finely chopped
- 2 garlic cloves, minced
- 1 cup arborio rice
- 1½ teaspoons kosher salt, plus more to taste
- ½ cup dry white wine
- 2 ounces finely grated Parmesan
- ¼ cup heavy cream
- 1 teaspoon freshly ground black pepper, plus more to taste
- 3 ounces low-moisture mozzarella, cut into ⅓-inch pieces
- 1½ cups panko breadcrumbs
- 2 tablespoons melted salted butter
- ½ cup all-purpose flour 2 large eggs, beaten Cooking spray
- Marinara sauce, for serving

Directions:

1. Simmer chicken stock in a pot, then keep warm on low heat.
2. Heat 2 tablespoons of unsalted butter in a medium saucepan over medium heat.
3. Add onions to the saucepan and cook for 5 minutes or until softened.
4. Add garlic and cook for 1 minute or until softened.
5. Add rice and 1½ teaspoons of kosher salt to the saucepan.
6. Cook the rice for 3 minutes or until the edges turn translucent.
7. Pour in the wine, stir, and cook for 3 minutes or until the wine is all evaporated and the rice looks dry.
8. Ladle in 1 cup of the warm chicken stock and bring to a simmer. Stirring often, cook the rice for 5 minutes or until liquid is absorbed. Repeat this process with another cup of chicken stock.

9. Add the remaining 1½ cups of chicken stock and cook, stirring often, for 10 minutes or until the rice is cooked through but toothsome and the liquid is mostly absorbed.
10. Remove the risotto from the heat and mix in Parmesan, heavy cream, black pepper, and the remaining two tablespoons of unsalted butter.
11. Season the risotto to taste with salt and black pepper.
12. Spread risotto in an even layer on a parchment-lined baking sheet and cover with plastic wrap.
13. Place the risotto in the fridge and chill for 4 hours.
14. Seperate the chilled risotto into 14 even pieces and form them into round patties about 2½ inches in diameter.
15. Place a piece of mozzarella in the center of a patty, pinch and shape the risotto so it completely encases the cheese, then roll into a ball. Repeat with each risotto patty.
16. Place the balls onto the baking sheet lined with fresh parchment paper, cover with plastic wrap, and place in the freezer for 15 minutes.
17. Place the panko breadcrumbs into a food processor and pulse until finely ground, then place into a bowl.
18. Mix the panko breadcrumbs with the melted salted butter until well combined.
19. Remove the risotto balls from the freezer and dredge in flour, dip in beaten eggs, then cover with breadcrumbs. Repeat this process with the rest of the balls. Set aside.
20. Preheat the toaster oven to 400°F.
21. Place the balls into the fry basket, spray them liberally with cooking spray, then insert the basket at mid position in the preheated oven.
22. Select the Air Fry function, adjust time to 20 minutes, and press Start/Pause.
23. Remove the arancini from the oven and serve with marinara sauce.

Sugar-glazed Walnuts

Servings: 6

Cooking Time: 5 Minutes

Ingredients:

- 1 Large egg white(s)
- 2 tablespoons Granulated white sugar
- ⅛ teaspoon Table salt
- 2 cups (7 ounces) Walnut halves

Directions:

1. Preheat the toaster oven to 400°F.
2. Use a whisk to beat the egg white(s) in a large bowl until quite foamy, more so than just well combined but certainly not yet a meringue.
3. If you're working with the quantities for a small batch, remove half of the foamy egg white.
4. If you're working with the quantities for a large batch, remove a quarter of it. It's fine to eyeball the amounts.
5. You can store the removed egg white in a sealed container to save for another use.
6. Stir in the sugar and salt. Add the walnut halves and toss to coat evenly and well, including the nuts' crevasses.
7. When the machine is at temperature, use a slotted spoon to transfer the walnut halves to the air fryer oven, taking care not to dislodge any coating. Gently spread the nuts into as close to one layer as you can. Air-fry undisturbed for 2 minutes.
8. Break up any clumps, toss the walnuts gently but well, and air-fry for 3 minutes more, tossing after 1 minute, then every 30 seconds thereafter, until the nuts are browned in spots and very aromatic. Watch carefully so they don't burn.
9. Gently dump the nuts onto a lipped baking sheet and spread them into one layer. Cool for at least 10 minutes before serving, separating any that stick together. The walnuts can be stored in a sealed container at room temperature for up to 5 days.

Polenta Fries With Chili-lime Mayo

Servings: 4

Cooking Time: 28 Minutes

Ingredients:

- 2 teaspoons vegetable or olive oil
- ¼ teaspoon paprika
- 1 pound prepared polenta, cut into 3-inch x ½-inch sticks
- salt and freshly ground black pepper
- Chili-Lime Mayo
- ½ cup mayonnaise
- 1 teaspoon chili powder
- ¼ teaspoon ground cumin
- juice of half a lime
- 1 teaspoon chopped fresh cilantro
- salt and freshly ground black pepper

Directions:

1. Preheat the toaster oven to 400°F.
2. Combine the oil and paprika and then carefully toss the polenta sticks in the mixture.
3. Air-fry the polenta fries at 400°F for 15 minutes. Rotate the fries and continue to air-fry for another 13 minutes or until the fries have browned nicely. Season to taste with salt and freshly ground black pepper.
4. To make the chili-lime mayo, combine all the ingredients in a small bowl and stir well.
5. Serve the polenta fries warm with chili-lime mayo on the side for dipping.

Cheesy Zucchini Squash Casserole

Servings: 12-14

Cooking Time: 30 Minutes

Ingredients:

- 1 Tablespoon olive oil
- 1 medium sweet onion, halved and thinly sliced
- 1 garlic clove, minced
- 1 pound zucchini, thinly sliced
- 1 pound yellow squash, thinly sliced
- 1 large egg
- 1/2 cup sour cream
- 1 cup shredded Cheddar cheese
- 1 cup shredded Swiss cheese
- 1 teaspoon thyme
- 1 teaspoon salt
- 1/2 teaspoon black pepper
- 3/4 cup seasoned panko crumbs
- 1 Tablespoon butter, melted

Directions:

1. Preheat the toaster oven to 350°F.
2. Heat olive oil in large skillet over medium-high heat. Add onion and garlic; cook 2 minutes. Stir in zucchini and yellow squash, cooking an additional 4 minutes or until squash is tender.
3. Beat egg and sour cream in large bowl until well blended. Stir in squash mixture, cheeses, thyme, salt and pepper. Pour into 8x8-inch baking dish.
4. Stir crumbs and butter in small bowl. Sprinkle over squash mixture.
5. Bake 25 to 30 minutes or until crumbs are golden brown and mixture is heated through.

Sausage Cheese Pinwheels

Servings: 16

Cooking Time: 22 Minutes

Ingredients:

- 1 sheet frozen puff pastry, about 9 inches square, thawed (½ of a 17.3-ounce package)
- ½ pound bulk sausage
- ¾ cup shredded cheddar cheese

Directions:

1. Preheat the toaster oven to 400°F. Grease a 12 x 12-inch baking pan.
2. Unfold the puff pastry on a lightly floured surface and roll into a 10 x 12-inch rectangle. Carefully spread the sausage over the surface of the rectangle to within ½ inch of all four edges. Sprinkle the cheese evenly over the sausage. Starting with the long side, roll up tightly and press the edges to seal.
3. Using a serrated knife, slice the roll into ½-inch-thick pieces. You will get about 16 slices. Place the slices, cut side up, in the prepared baking pan. Bake for 18 to 22 minutes or until golden and the sausage is cooked through.
4. Serve warm or at room temperature.

Cauliflower "tater" Tots

Servings: 6

Cooking Time: 10 Minutes

Ingredients:

- 1 head of cauliflower
- 2 eggs
- ¼ cup all-purpose flour
- ½ cup grated Parmesan cheese
- 1 teaspoon salt
- freshly ground black pepper
- vegetable or olive oil, in a spray bottle

Directions:

1. Grate the head of cauliflower with a box grater or finely chop it in a food processor. You should have about 3½ cups. Place the chopped cauliflower in the center of a clean kitchen towel and twist the towel tightly to squeeze all the water out of the cauliflower. (This can be done in two batches to make it easier to drain all the water from the cauliflower.)
2. Place the squeezed cauliflower in a large bowl. Add the eggs, flour, Parmesan cheese, salt and freshly ground black pepper. Shape the cauliflower into small cylinders or "tater tot" shapes, rolling roughly one tablespoon of the mixture at a time. Place the tots on a cookie sheet lined with paper towel to absorb any residual moisture. Spray the cauliflower tots all over with oil.
3. Preheat the toaster oven to 400°F.
4. Air-fry the tots at 400°F, one layer at a time for 10 minutes, turning them over for the last few minutes of the cooking process for even browning. Season with salt and black pepper. Serve hot with your favorite dipping sauce.

Sheet Pan Chicken Nachos

Servings: 2

Cooking Time: 20 Minutes

Ingredients:

- Tortilla chips
- 2 cups shredded chicken
- 1 3/4 cup Fresh & Spicy Salsa, divided
- 1 cup drained black beans
- 1 package (2 cups) shredded colby and Monterey Jack cheese, divided
- 1 fresh jalapeno, sliced
- Guacamole

Directions:

1. Heat toaster oven to 350°F. Line a toaster oven pan with aluminum foil and spray foil with nonstick cooking spray.
2. Arrange tortilla chips in an even layer in pan.
3. In a small bowl, combine chicken, 3/4 cup salsa, black beans and 1 cup shredded cheese.
4. Spoon chicken mixture over chips. Top with remaining cheese and jalapeno slices.
5. Bake until cheese is melted and mixture is heated through, 18 to 20 minutes
6. Serve with remaining salsa and guacamole.

Cinnamon Apple Chips

Servings: 4

Cooking Time: 480 Minutes

Ingredients:

- 1 apple
- 1 tablespoon lemon juice
- ¼ teaspoon cinnamon

Directions:

1. Slice the apple into ⅛-inch-thick slices, preferably by using a mandoline slicer.
2. Place slices in a bowl of water mixed with the lemon juice to prevent browning. Remove after 2 minutes and dry thoroughly with paper towels.
3. Sprinkle the apple slices with cinnamon and place on the food tray.
4. Insert the food tray at mid position in the preheated oven.
5. Preheat the toaster oven to 130°F.
6. Remove when apple chips are crispy.

Baba Ghanouj

Servings: 2

Cooking Time: 40 Minutes

Ingredients:

- 2 Small (12-ounce) purple Italian eggplant(s)
- ¼ cup Olive oil
- ¼ cup Tahini
- ½ teaspoon Ground black pepper
- ¼ teaspoon Onion powder
- ¼ teaspoon Mild smoked paprika (optional)
- Up to 1 teaspoon Table salt

Directions:

1. Preheat the toaster oven to 400°F.
2. Prick the eggplant(s) on all sides with a fork. When the machine is at temperature, set the eggplant(s) in the air fryer oven in one layer. Air-fry undisturbed for 40 minutes, or until blackened and soft.
3. Remove from the machine. Cool the eggplant(s) in the air fryer oven for 20 minutes.
4. Use a nonstick-safe spatula, and perhaps a flatware tablespoon for balance, to gently transfer the eggplant(s) to a bowl. The juices will run out. Make sure the bowl is close to the air fryer oven. Split the eggplant(s) open.
5. Scrape the soft insides of half an eggplant into a food processor. Repeat with the remaining piece(s). Add any juices from the bowl to the eggplant in the food processor, but discard the skins and stems.
6. Add the olive oil, tahini, pepper, onion powder, and smoked paprika (if using). Add about half the salt, then cover and process until smooth, stopping the machine at least once to scrape down the inside of the canister. Check the spread for salt and add more as needed. Scrape the baba ghanouj into a bowl and serve warm, or set aside at room temperature for up to 2 hours, or cover and store in the refrigerator for up to 4 days.

Sesame Green Beans

Servings: 4

Cooking Time: 8 Minutes

Ingredients:

- 1 pound green beans, stems trimmed
- 1 tablespoon olive oil
- 1 teaspoon sesame oil
- 1 tablespoon sesame seeds
- Pinch sea salt

Directions:

1. Preheat the toaster oven to 350°F on AIR FRY for 5 minutes.
2. In a large bowl, toss the green beans, olive oil, and sesame oil.
3. Place the air-fryer basket in the baking tray and spread the beans in the basket.
4. Place the tray in position 2 and air fry for 8 minutes, shaking the basket at the halfway point. The beans should be lightly golden and fragrant.
5. Transfer the beans to a serving plate and serve topped with the sesame seeds and seasoned with salt.

FISH AND SEAFOOD

Almond-crusted Fish

Servings: 4

Cooking Time: 10 Minutes

Ingredients:

- 4 4-ounce fish fillets
- ¾ cup breadcrumbs
- ¼ cup sliced almonds, crushed
- 2 tablespoons lemon juice
- ⅛ teaspoon cayenne
- salt and pepper
- ¾ cup flour
- 1 egg, beaten with 1 tablespoon water
- oil for misting or cooking spray

Directions:

1. Split fish fillets lengthwise down the center to create 8 pieces.
2. Mix breadcrumbs and almonds together and set aside.
3. Mix the lemon juice and cayenne together. Brush on all sides of fish.
4. Season fish to taste with salt and pepper.
5. Place the flour on a sheet of wax paper.
6. Roll fillets in flour, dip in egg wash, and roll in the crumb mixture.
7. Mist both sides of fish with oil or cooking spray.
8. Spray air fryer oven and lay fillets inside.
9. Air-fry at 390°F for 5 minutes, turn fish over, and air-fry for an additional 5 minutes or until fish is done and flakes easily.

Horseradish Crusted Salmon

Servings: 2

Cooking Time: 14 Minutes

Ingredients:

- 2 (5-ounce) salmon fillets
- salt and freshly ground black pepper
- 2 teaspoons Dijon mustard
- ½ cup panko breadcrumbs
- 2 tablespoons prepared horseradish
- ½ teaspoon finely chopped lemon zest
- 1 tablespoon olive oil
- 1 tablespoon chopped fresh parsley

Directions:

1. Preheat the toaster oven to 360°F.
2. Season the salmon with salt and freshly ground black pepper. Then spread the Dijon mustard on the salmon, coating the entire surface.
3. Combine the breadcrumbs, horseradish, lemon zest and olive oil in a small bowl. Spread the mixture over the top of the salmon and press down lightly with your hands, adhering it to the salmon using the mustard as "glue".
4. Transfer the salmon to the air fryer oven and air-fry at 360°F for 14 minutes (depending on how thick your fillet is) or until the fish feels firm to the touch. Sprinkle with the parsley.

Skewered Salsa Verde Shrimp

Servings: 4

Cooking Time: 8 Minutes

Ingredients:

- 1½ pounds large fresh shrimp, peeled and deveined
- Brushing mixture:
- 1 7-ounce can salsa verde
- 1 teaspoon ground cumin
- ½ teaspoon chopped fresh cilantro or parsley
- 1 teaspoon garlic powder
- 3 tablespoons plain yogurt
- 1 tablespoon olive oil
- Lemon wedges

Directions:

1. Thread the shrimp onto the skewers.
2. Combine the brushing mixture ingredients in a small bowl. Adjust the seasonings and brush the shrimp with the mixture.
3. BROIL the shrimp for 4 minutes. Turn the skewers, brush the shrimp again, and broil for another 4 minutes, or until the shrimp are firm and cooked. Remove the shrimp from the skewers and serve with lemon wedges.

Fish And "chips"

Servings: 2

Cooking Time: 10 Minutes

Ingredients:

- ½ cup flour
- ½ teaspoon paprika
- ¼ teaspoon ground white pepper (or freshly ground black pepper)
- 1 egg
- ¼ cup mayonnaise
- 2 cups salt & vinegar kettle cooked potato chips, coarsely crushed
- 12 ounces cod
- tartar sauce
- lemon wedges

Directions:

1. Set up a dredging station. Combine the flour, paprika and pepper in a shallow dish. Combine the egg and mayonnaise in a second shallow dish. Place the crushed potato chips in a third shallow dish.
2. Cut the cod into 6 pieces. Dredge each piece of fish in the flour, then dip it into the egg mixture and then place it into the crushed potato chips. Make sure all sides of the fish are covered and pat the chips gently onto the fish so they stick well.
3. Preheat the toaster oven to 370°F.
4. Place the coated fish fillets into the air fry oven. (It is ok if a couple of pieces slightly overlap or rest on top of other fillets in order to fit everything in the air fryer oven.)
5. Air-fry for 10 minutes, gently turning the fish over halfway through the cooking time.
6. Transfer the fish to a platter and serve with tartar sauce and lemon wedges.

Tex-mex Fish Tacos

Servings: 3

Cooking Time: 7 Minutes

Ingredients:

- ¾ teaspoon Chile powder
- ¼ teaspoon Ground cumin
- ¼ teaspoon Dried oregano
- 3 5-ounce skinless mahi-mahi fillets
- Vegetable oil spray
- 3 Corn or flour tortillas
- 6 tablespoons Diced tomatoes
- 3 tablespoons Regular, low-fat, or fat-free sour cream

Directions:

1. Preheat the toaster oven to 400°F.
2. Stir the chile powder, cumin, and oregano in a small bowl until well combined.
3. Coat each piece of fish all over (even the sides and ends) with vegetable oil spray. Sprinkle the spice mixture evenly over all sides of the fillets. Lightly spray them again.
4. When the machine is at temperature, set the fillets in the air fryer oven with as much air space between them as possible. Air-fry undisturbed for 7 minutes, until lightly browned and firm but not hard.
5. Use a nonstick-safe spatula to transfer the fillets to a wire rack. Microwave the tortillas on high for a few seconds, until supple. Put a fillet in each tortilla and top each with 2 tablespoons diced tomatoes and 1 tablespoon sour cream.

Beer-breaded Halibut Fish Tacos

Servings: 4

Cooking Time: 10 Minutes

Ingredients:

- 1 pound halibut, cut into 1-inch strips
- 1 cup light beer
- 1 jalapeño, minced and divided
- 1 clove garlic, minced
- ¼ teaspoon ground cumin
- ½ cup cornmeal
- ¼ cup all-purpose flour
- 1¼ teaspoons sea salt, divided
- 2 cups shredded cabbage
- 1 lime, juiced and divided
- ¼ cup Greek yogurt
- ¼ cup mayonnaise
- 1 cup grape tomatoes, quartered
- ½ cup chopped cilantro
- ¼ cup chopped onion
- 1 egg, whisked
- 8 corn tortillas

Directions:

1. In a shallow baking dish, place the fish, the beer, 1 teaspoon of the minced jalapeño, the garlic, and the cumin. Cover and refrigerate for 30 minutes.
2. Meanwhile, in a medium bowl, mix together the cornmeal, flour, and ½ teaspoon of the salt.
3. In large bowl, mix together the shredded cabbage, 1 tablespoon of the lime juice, the Greek yogurt, the mayonnaise, and ½ teaspoon of the salt.
4. In a small bowl, make the pico de gallo by mixing together the tomatoes, cilantro, onion, ¼ teaspoon of the salt, the remaining jalapeño, and the remaining lime juice.
5. Remove the fish from the refrigerator and discard the marinade. Dredge the fish in the whisked egg; then dredge the fish in the cornmeal flour mixture, until all pieces of fish have been breaded.
6. Preheat the toaster oven to 350°F.
7. Place the fish in the air fryer oven and spray liberally with cooking spray. Air-fry for 6 minutes, flip the fish, and cook another 4 minutes.
8. While the fish is cooking, heat the tortillas in a heavy skillet for 1 to 2 minutes over high heat.
9. To assemble the tacos, place the battered fish on the heated tortillas, and top with slaw and pico de gallo. Serve immediately.

Molasses-glazed Salmon

Servings: 4

Cooking Time: 15 Minutes

Ingredients:

- Oil spray (hand-pumped)
- 4 (5-ounce) salmon fillets
- Sea salt, for seasoning
- ¼ cup molasses
- 1 teaspoon fresh ginger, peeled and grated

Directions:

1. Preheat the toaster oven to 350°F on CONVECTION BAKE for 5 minutes.
2. Place the air-fryer basket in the baking tray. Generously spray the basket with the oil.
3. Pat the salmon dry with paper towels, season lightly with salt, and place on the baking tray.
4. In a small bowl, stir the molasses and ginger until well blended.
5. Spread the molasses mixture on the fish fillets.
6. Place the baking tray in position 2 and bake for 15 minutes until just cooked through. Serve.

Oysters Broiled In Wine Sauce

Servings: 2

Cooking Time: 20 Minutes

Ingredients:

- Sauce:
- 2 tablespoons margarine, at room temperature
- 1 cup dry white wine
- 3 garlic cloves, minced
- Salt and freshly ground black pepper to taste
- 24 fresh oysters, shucked and drained

Directions:

1. Combine the sauce ingredients in a 1-quart 8½ × 8½ × 4-inch ovenproof baking dish and adjust the seasonings to taste.
2. BROIL the sauce for 5 minutes, remove the pan from the oven, and stir. Return to the oven and broil for another 5 minutes, or until the sauce begins to bubble. Remove from the oven and cool for 5 minutes. Add the oysters, spooning the sauce over them to cover thoroughly.
3. BROIL for 5 minutes, or until the oysters are just cooked.

Garlic-lemon Shrimp Skewers

Servings: 2

Cooking Time: 8 Minutes

Ingredients:

- Juice and zest of 1 lemon
- 1 tablespoon olive oil
- ½ teaspoon garlic puree
- ¼ teaspoon smoked paprika
- 12 large shrimp, peeled and deveined
- Oil spray (hand-pumped)
- Sea salt, for seasoning
- Freshly ground black pepper, for seasoning
- 1 tablespoon chopped fresh parsley

Directions:

1. Preheat the toaster oven to 350°F on AIR FRY for 5 minutes.
2. In a medium bowl, stir the lemon juice, lemon zest, olive oil, garlic, and paprika.
3. Add the shrimp and toss to combine. Cover, refrigerate, and let marinate for 30 minutes.
4. Soak 4 wooden skewers in water while the shrimp marinate.
5. Place the air-fryer basket in the baking tray and spray it generously with the oil.
6. Thread 3 shrimp on each skewer and place them in the basket. Discard any remaining marinade.
7. In position 2, air fry for 8 minutes, turning halfway through, until just cooked.
8. Season with the salt and pepper and serve topped with the parsley.

Tilapia Teriyaki

Servings: 3

Cooking Time: 10 Minutes

Ingredients:

- 4 tablespoons teriyaki sauce
- 1 tablespoon pineapple juice
- 1 pound tilapia fillets
- cooking spray
- 6 ounces frozen mixed peppers with onions, thawed and drained
- 2 cups cooked rice

Directions:

1. Mix the teriyaki sauce and pineapple juice together in a small bowl.
2. Split tilapia fillets down the center lengthwise.
3. Brush all sides of fish with the sauce, spray air fryer oven with nonstick cooking spray, and place fish in the air fryer oven.
4. Stir the peppers and onions into the remaining sauce and spoon over the fish. Save any leftover sauce for drizzling over the fish when serving.
5. Air-fry at 360°F for 10 minutes, until fish flakes easily with a fork and is done in center.
6. Divide into 3 or 4 servings and serve each with approximately ½ cup cooked rice.

Fried Shrimp

Servings: 3

Cooking Time: 7 Minutes

Ingredients:

- 1 Large egg white
- 2 tablespoons Water
- 1 cup Plain dried bread crumbs (gluten-free, if a concern)
- ¼ cup All-purpose flour or almond flour
- ¼ cup Yellow cornmeal
- 1 teaspoon Celery salt
- 1 teaspoon Mild paprika
- Up to ½ teaspoon Cayenne (optional)
- ¾ pound Large shrimp (20–25 per pound), peeled and deveined
- Vegetable oil spray

Directions:

1. Preheat the toaster oven to 400°F.
2. Set two medium or large bowls on your counter. In the first, whisk the egg white and water until foamy. In the second, stir the bread crumbs, flour, cornmeal, celery salt, paprika, and cayenne (if using) until well combined.
3. Pour all the shrimp into the egg white mixture and stir gently until all the shrimp are coated. Use kitchen tongs to pick them up one by one and transfer them to the bread-crumb mixture. Turn each in the bread-crumb mixture to coat it evenly and thoroughly on all sides before setting it on a cutting board. When you're done coating the shrimp, coat them all on both sides with the vegetable oil spray.
4. Set the shrimp in as close to one layer in the air fryer oven as you can. Some may overlap. Air-fry for 7 minutes, gently rearranging the shrimp at the 4-minute mark to get covered surfaces exposed, until golden brown and firm but not hard.
5. Use kitchen tongs to gently transfer the shrimp to a wire rack. Cool for only a minute or two before serving.

Crab Cakes

Servings: 4

Cooking Time: 9 Minutes

Ingredients:

- 1 pound lump crab meat, checked for shells
- ⅓ cup breadcrumbs
- ¼ cup finely chopped onions
- ¼ cup finely chopped red bell peppers
- ¼ cup finely chopped parsley
- ¼ teaspoon sea salt
- 2 eggs, whisked
- ¾ cup mayonnaise, divided
- ¼ cup sour cream
- 1 lemon, divided
- ¼ cup sweet pickle relish
- 1 tablespoon prepared mustard

Directions:

1. In a large bowl, mix together the crab meat, breadcrumbs, onions, bell peppers, parsley, sea salt, eggs, and ¼ cup of the mayonnaise.
2. Preheat the toaster oven to 380°F.
3. Form 8 patties with the crab cake mixture. Line the air fryer oven with parchment paper and place the crab cakes on the parchment paper. Spray with cooking spray. Air-fry for 4 minutes, turn over the crab cakes, spray with cooking spray, and air-fry for an additional 3 to 5 minutes, or until golden brown and the edges are crispy. Cook in batches as needed.
4. Meanwhile, make the sauce. In a small bowl, mix together the remaining ½ cup of mayonnaise, the sour cream, the juice from ½ of the lemon, the pickle relish, and the mustard.
5. Place the cooked crab cakes on a serving platter and serve with the remaining ½ lemon cut into wedges and the dipping sauce.

Roasted Pepper Tilapia

Servings: 6

Cooking Time: 20 Minutes

Ingredients:

- 6 5-ounce tilapia fillets
- 2 tablespoons olive oil
- Filling:
- 1 cucumber, peeled, seeds scooped out and discarded, and chopped
- ½ cup chopped roasted peppers, drained
- 2 tablespoons lemon juice
- 2 tablespoons chopped fresh parsley or cilantro
- 1 teaspoon garlic powder
- 1 teaspoon paprika
- Salt and freshly ground black pepper to taste
- Dip mixture:
- 1 cup nonfat sour cream
- 2 tablespoons low-fat mayonnaise
- 3 tablespoons Dijon mustard
- 1 teaspoon Worcestershire sauce
- 1 teaspoon dried dill

Directions:

1. Combine the filling ingredients in a bowl, adjusting the seasonings to taste.
2. Spoon equal portions of filling in the centers of the tilapia filets. Roll up the fillets, starting at the smallest end. Secure each roll with toothpicks and place the rolls in an oiled or nonstick baking pan. Carefully brush the fillets with oil and place them in an oiled or nonstick 8½ × 8½ × 2-inch square baking (cake) pan.
3. BROIL for 20 minutes, or until the fillets are lightly browned. Combine the dip mixture ingredients in a small bowl and serve with the fish.

BEEF PORK AND LAMB

Lamb Curry

Servings: 4

Cooking Time: 40 Minutes

Ingredients:

- 1 pound lean lamb for stewing, trimmed and cut into 1 × 1-inch pieces
- 1 small onion, chopped
- 3 garlic cloves, minced
- 2 plum tomatoes, chopped
- ½ cup dry white wine
- 2 tablespoons curry powder
- Salt and cayenne to taste

Directions:

1. Preheat the toaster oven to 400° F.
2. Combine all the ingredients in an 8½ × 8½ × 4-inch ovenproof baking dish. Adjust the seasonings.
3. BAKE, covered, for 40 minutes, or until the meat is tender and the onion is cooked.

Perfect Pork Chops

Servings: 3

Cooking Time: 10 Minutes

Ingredients:

- ¾ teaspoon Mild paprika
- ¾ teaspoon Dried thyme
- ¾ teaspoon Onion powder
- ¼ teaspoon Garlic powder
- ¼ teaspoon Table salt
- ¼ teaspoon Ground black pepper
- 3 6-ounce boneless center-cut pork loin chops
- Vegetable oil spray

Directions:

1. Preheat the toaster oven to 400°F.
2. Mix the paprika, thyme, onion powder, garlic powder, salt, and pepper in a small bowl until well combined. Massage this mixture into both sides of the chops. Generously coat both sides of the chops with vegetable oil spray.
3. When the machine is at temperature, set the chops in the air fryer oven with as much air space between them as possible. Air-fry undisturbed for 10 minutes, or until an instant-read meat thermometer inserted into the thickest part of a chop registers 145°F.
4. Use kitchen tongs to transfer the chops to a cutting board or serving plates. Cool for 5 minutes before serving.

Sloppy Joes

Servings: 4

Cooking Time: 17 Minutes

Ingredients:

- oil for misting or cooking spray
- 1 pound very lean ground beef
- 1 teaspoon onion powder
- ⅓ cup ketchup
- ¼ cup water
- ½ teaspoon celery seed
- 1 tablespoon lemon juice
- 1½ teaspoons brown sugar
- 1¼ teaspoons low-sodium Worcestershire sauce
- ½ teaspoon salt (optional)
- ½ teaspoon vinegar
- ⅛ teaspoon dry mustard
- hamburger or slider buns

Directions:

1. Spray air fryer oven with nonstick cooking spray or olive oil.
2. Break raw ground beef into small chunks and pile into air fryer oven.
3. Air-fry at 390°F for 5 minutes. Stir to break apart and cook 3 minutes. Stir and cook 4 minutes longer or until meat is well done.
4. Remove meat from air fryer oven, drain, and use a knife and fork to crumble into small pieces.
5. Give your air fryer oven a quick rinse to remove any bits of meat.
6. Place all the remaining ingredients except the buns in a 6 x 6-inch baking pan and mix together.
7. Add meat and stir well.
8. Air-fry at 330°F for 5 minutes. Stir and air-fry for 2 minutes.
9. Scoop onto buns.

Lamb Burger With Feta And Olives

Servings: 3

Cooking Time: 16 Minutes

Ingredients:

- 2 teaspoons olive oil
- ⅓ onion, finely chopped
- 1 clove garlic, minced
- 1 pound ground lamb
- 2 tablespoons fresh parsley, finely chopped
- 1½ teaspoons fresh oregano, finely chopped
- ½ cup black olives, finely chopped
- ⅓ cup crumbled feta cheese
- ½ teaspoon salt
- freshly ground black pepper
- 4 thick pita breads
- toppings and condiments

Directions:

1. Preheat a medium skillet over medium-high heat on the stovetop. Add the olive oil and cook the onion until tender, but not browned – about 4 to 5 minutes. Add the garlic and air-fry for another minute. Transfer the onion and garlic to a mixing bowl and add the ground lamb, parsley, oregano, olives, feta cheese, salt and pepper. Gently mix the ingredients together.
2. Divide the mixture into 3 or 4 equal portions and then form the hamburgers, being careful not to over-handle the meat. One good way to do this is to throw the meat back and forth between your hands like a baseball, packing the meat each time you catch it. Flatten the balls into patties, making an indentation in the center of each patty. Flatten the sides of the patties as well to make it easier to fit them into the air fryer oven.
3. Preheat the toaster oven to 370°F.
4. If you don't have room for all four burgers, air-fry two or three burgers at a time for 8 minutes at 370°F. Flip the burgers over and air-fry for another 8 minutes. If you cooked your burgers in batches, return the first batch of burgers to the air fryer oven for the last two minutes of cooking to re-heat. This should give you a medium-well burger. If you'd prefer a medium-rare burger, shorten the cooking time to about 13 minutes. Remove the burgers to a resting plate and let the burgers rest for a few minutes before dressing and serving.
5. While the burgers are resting, toast the pita breads in the air fryer oven for 2 minutes. Tuck the burgers into the toasted pita breads, or wrap the pitas around the burgers and serve with a tzatziki sauce or some mayonnaise.

Seasoned Boneless Pork Sirloin Chops

Servings: 2

Cooking Time: 16 Minutes

Ingredients:

- Seasoning mixture:
- ½ teaspoon ground cumin
- ¼ teaspoon turmeric
- Pinch of ground cardamom
- Pinch of grated nutmeg
- 1 teaspoon vegetable oil
- 1 teaspoon Pickapeppa sauce
- 2½- to ¾-pound boneless lean pork sirloin chops

Directions:

1. Combine the seasoning mixture ingredients in a small bowl and brush on both sides of the chops. Place the chops on the broiling rack with a pan underneath.
2. BROIL 8 minutes, remove the chops, turn, and brush with the mixture. Broil again for 8 minutes, or until the chops are done to your preference.

Smokehouse-style Beef Ribs

Servings: 3

Cooking Time: 25 Minutes

Ingredients:

- ¼ teaspoon Mild smoked paprika
- ¼ teaspoon Garlic powder
- ¼ teaspoon Onion powder
- ¼ teaspoon Table salt
- ¼ teaspoon Ground black pepper
- 3 10- to 12-ounce beef back ribs (not beef short ribs)

Directions:

1. Preheat the toaster oven to 350°F .
2. Mix the smoked paprika, garlic powder, onion powder, salt, and pepper in a small bowl until uniform. Massage and pat this mixture onto the ribs.
3. When the machine is at temperature, set the ribs in the air fryer oven in one layer, turning them on their sides if necessary, sort of like they're spooning but with at least ¼ inch air space between them. Air-fry for 25 minutes, turning once, until deep brown and sizzling.
4. Use kitchen tongs to transfer the ribs to a wire rack. Cool for 5 minutes before serving.

Beef Bourguignon

Servings: 6

Cooking Time: 240 Minutes

Ingredients:

- 4 slices bacon, chopped into ½-inch pieces
- 3 pounds chuck roast, cut into 2-inch chunks
- 1 tablespoon kosher salt, plus more to taste
- 1½ tablespoons black pepper, plus more to taste
- 4 tablespoons all purpose flour, divided
- 2 tablespoons olive oil
- 2 large carrots, cut into ½-inch thick slices
- ½ large white onion, diced
- 4 cloves garlic, minced
- 2 tablespoons tomato paste
- 3 cups red wine (Merlot, Pinot Noir, or Chianti)
- 2 cups beef stock
- 1 beef bouillon cube, crushed
- ½ teaspoon dried thyme
- ¼ teaspoon dried parsley
- 2 bay leaves
- 10 ounces fresh small white or brown mushrooms, quartered
- 2 tablespoons cornstarch (optional)
- 2 tablespoons water (optional)

Directions:

1. Render the bacon in a large pot over medium heat for 5 minutes or until crispy.
2. Drain the bacon and set aside, leaving the bacon fat in the pot.
3. Mix together chuck roast chunks, kosher salt, black pepper, and 2 tablespoons of all purpose flour until well combined.
4. Dredge the beef of any extra flour and sear in the bacon grease for about 4 minutes on each side. It is important not to overcrowd the pot, so you may need to work in batches.
5. Remove the beef when done and set aside with the bacon.
6. Add the olive oil, sliced carrots, and diced onion to the pot. Cook for 5 minutes, then add the garlic and cook for another minute.
7. Add the tomato paste and cook for 1 minute, then mix in the remaining 2 tablespoons of flour and cook on medium low for 4 minutes.
8. Pour in the wine and beef stock, scraping the bottom of the pot to make sure there aren't any bits stuck to the bottom.
9. Add the bacon and seared meat back into the pot, along with the bouillon cube, dried thyme, dried parsley, bay leaves, and mushrooms. Mix well and bring to a light boil.
10. Insert the wire rack at low position in the Air Fryer Toaster Oven.

11. Cover the pot with foil and place on the rack in the oven. Make sure the foil is secure so it doesn't lift and contact the heating elements.
12. Select the Slow Cook function, adjust time to 4 hours, and press Start/Pause.
13. Remove the pot carefully from the oven when done and place back on the stove.
14. Discard the foil, mix the stew, and season to taste with salt and pepper.
15. Thicken the stew if desired by using a cornstarch slurry of 2 tablespoons cornstarch and 2 tablespoons water. Add half, mix, and bring to a boil, stirring occasionally. If the sauce is still too thin, add the other half of the slurry.

Almond And Sun-dried Tomato Crusted Pork Chops

Servings: 4

Cooking Time: 10 Minutes

Ingredients:

- ½ cup oil-packed sun-dried tomatoes
- ½ cup toasted almonds
- ¼ cup grated Parmesan cheese
- ½ cup olive oil
- 2 tablespoons water
- ½ teaspoon salt
- freshly ground black pepper
- 4 center-cut boneless pork chops (about 1¼ pounds)

Directions:

1. Place the sun-dried tomatoes into a food processor and pulse them until they are coarsely chopped. Add the almonds, Parmesan cheese, olive oil, water, salt and pepper. Process all the ingredients into a smooth paste. Spread most of the paste (leave a little in reserve) onto both sides of the pork chops and then pierce the meat several times with a needle-style meat tenderizer or a fork. Let the pork chops sit and marinate for at least 1 hour (refrigerate if marinating for longer than 1 hour).
2. Preheat the toaster oven to 370°F.
3. Brush a little olive oil on the bottom of the air fryer oven. Transfer the pork chops into the air fryer oven, spooning a little more of the sun-dried tomato paste onto the pork chops if there are any gaps where the paste may have been rubbed off. Air-fry the pork chops at 370°F for 10 minutes, turning the chops over halfway through the cooking process.
4. When the pork chops have finished cooking, transfer them to a serving plate and serve with mashed potatoes and vegetables for a hearty meal.

Vietnamese Beef Lettuce Wraps

Servings: 4

Cooking Time: 12 Minutes

Ingredients:

- ⅓ cup low-sodium soy sauce
- 2 teaspoons fish sauce
- 2 teaspoons brown sugar
- 1 tablespoon chili paste
- juice of 1 lime
- 2 cloves garlic, minced
- 2 teaspoons fresh ginger, minced
- 1 pound beef sirloin
- Sauce
- ⅓ cup low-sodium soy sauce
- juice of 2 limes
- 1 tablespoon mirin wine
- 2 teaspoons chili paste
- Serving
- 1 head butter lettuce
- ½ cup julienned carrots
- ½ cup julienned cucumber
- ½ cup sliced radishes, sliced into half moons
- 2 cups cooked rice noodles
- ⅓ cup chopped peanuts

Directions:

1. Combine the soy sauce, fish sauce, brown sugar, chili paste, lime juice, garlic and ginger in a bowl. Slice the beef into thin slices, then cut those slices in half. Add the beef to the marinade and marinate for 1 to 3 hours in the refrigerator. When you are ready to cook, remove the steak from the refrigerator and let it sit at room temperature for 30 minutes.
2. Preheat the toaster oven to 400°F.
3. Transfer the beef and marinade to the air fryer oven. Air-fry at 400°F for 12 minutes.
4. While the beef is cooking, prepare a wrap-building station. Combine the soy sauce, lime juice, mirin wine and chili paste in a bowl and transfer to a little pouring vessel. Separate the lettuce leaves from the head of lettuce and put them in a serving bowl. Place the carrots, cucumber, radish, rice noodles and chopped peanuts all in separate serving bowls.
5. When the beef has finished cooking, transfer it to another serving bowl and invite your guests to build their wraps. To build the wraps, place some beef in a lettuce leaf and top with carrots, cucumbers, some rice noodles and chopped peanuts. Drizzle a little sauce over top, fold the lettuce around the ingredients and enjoy!

Glazed Meatloaf

Servings: 4

Cooking Time: 60 Minutes

Ingredients:

- 2 pounds extra-lean ground beef
- ½ cup fine bread crumbs
- 1 large egg
- 1 medium carrot, shredded
- 2 teaspoons minced garlic
- ¼ cup milk
- 1 tablespoon Italian seasoning
- ½ teaspoon sea salt
- ⅛ teaspoon freshly ground black pepper
- ½ cup ketchup
- 1 tablespoon dark brown sugar
- 1 teaspoon apple cider vinegar

Directions:

1. Place the rack in position 1 and preheat the toaster oven to 375°F on BAKE for 5 minutes.
2. In a large bowl, mix the ground beef, bread crumbs, egg, carrot, garlic, milk, Italian seasoning, salt, and pepper until well combined.
3. Press the mixture into a 9-by-5-inch loaf pan.
4. In a small bowl, stir the ketchup, brown sugar, and vinegar. Set aside.
5. Bake for 40 minutes.
6. Take the meatloaf out and spread the glaze over the top. Bake an additional 20 minutes until cooked through, with an internal temperature of 165°F. Serve.

California Burritos

Servings: 4

Cooking Time: 17 Minutes

Ingredients:

- 1 pound sirloin steak, sliced thin
- 1 teaspoon dried oregano
- 1 teaspoon ground cumin
- ½ teaspoon garlic powder
- 16 tater tots
- ⅓ cup sour cream
- ½ lime, juiced
- 2 tablespoons hot sauce
- 1 large avocado, pitted
- 1 teaspoon salt, divided
- 4 large (8- to 10-inch) flour tortillas
- ½ cup shredded cheddar cheese or Monterey jack
- 2 tablespoons avocado oil

Directions:

1. Preheat the toaster oven to 380°F.
2. Season the steak with oregano, cumin, and garlic powder. Place the steak on one side of the air fryer oven and the tater tots on the other side. (It's okay for them to touch, because the flavors will all come together in the burrito.) Air-fry for 8 minutes, toss, and cook an additional 4 to 6 minutes.
3. Meanwhile, in a small bowl, stir together the sour cream, lime juice, and hot sauce.
4. In another small bowl, mash together the avocado and season with ½ teaspoon of the salt, to taste.
5. To assemble the burrito, lay out the tortillas, equally divide the meat amongst the tortillas. Season the steak equally with the remaining ½ teaspoon salt. Then layer the mashed avocado and sour cream mixture on top. Top each tortilla with 4 tater tots and finish each with 2 tablespoons cheese. Roll up the sides and, while holding in the sides, roll up the burrito. Place the burritos in the air fryer oven and brush with avocado oil (working in batches as needed); air-fry for 3 minutes or until lightly golden on the outside.

Barbecue-style London Broil

Servings: 5

Cooking Time: 17 Minutes

Ingredients:

- ¾ teaspoon Mild smoked paprika
- ¾ teaspoon Dried oregano
- ¾ teaspoon Table salt
- ¾ teaspoon Ground black pepper
- ¼ teaspoon Garlic powder
- ¼ teaspoon Onion powder
- 1½ pounds Beef London broil (in one piece)
- Olive oil spray

Directions:

1. Preheat the toaster oven to 400°F.
2. Mix the smoked paprika, oregano, salt, pepper, garlic powder, and onion powder in a small bowl until uniform.
3. Pat and rub this mixture across all surfaces of the beef. Lightly coat the beef on all sides with olive oil spray.
4. When the machine is at temperature, lay the London broil flat in the air fryer oven and air-fry undisturbed for 8 minutes for the small batch, 10 minutes for the medium batch, or 12 minutes for the large batch for medium-rare, until an instant-read meat thermometer inserted into the center of the meat registers 130°F (not USDA-approved). Add 1, 2, or 3 minutes, respectively (based on the size of the cut) for medium, until an instant-read meat thermometer registers 135°F (not USDA-approved). Or add 3, 4, or 5 minutes respectively for medium, until an instant-read meat thermometer registers 145°F (USDA-approved).
5. Use kitchen tongs to transfer the London broil to a cutting board. Let the meat rest for 10 minutes. It needs a long time for the juices to be reincorporated into the meat's fibers. Carve it against the grain into very thin (less than ¼-inch-thick) slices to serve.

Chicken Fried Steak

Servings: 4

Cooking Time: 15 Minutes

Ingredients:

- 2 eggs
- ½ cup buttermilk
- 1½ cups flour
- ¾ teaspoon salt
- ½ teaspoon pepper
- 1 pound beef cube steaks
- salt and pepper
- oil for misting or cooking spray

Directions:

1. Beat together eggs and buttermilk in a shallow dish.
2. In another shallow dish, stir together the flour, ½ teaspoon salt, and ¼ teaspoon pepper.
3. Season cube steaks with remaining salt and pepper to taste. Dip in flour, buttermilk egg wash, and then flour again.
4. Spray both sides of steaks with oil or cooking spray.
5. Cooking in 2 batches, place steaks in air fryer oven in single layer. Air-fry at 360°F for 10 minutes. Spray tops of steaks with oil and cook 5 minutes or until meat is well done.
6. Repeat to cook remaining steaks.

POULTRY

Teriyaki Chicken Drumsticks

Servings: 2

Cooking Time: 17 Minutes

Ingredients:

- 2 tablespoons soy sauce
- ¼ cup dry sherry
- 1 tablespoon brown sugar
- 2 tablespoons water
- 1 tablespoon rice wine vinegar
- 1 clove garlic, crushed
- 1-inch fresh ginger, peeled and sliced
- pinch crushed red pepper flakes
- 4 to 6 bone-in, skin-on chicken drumsticks
- 1 tablespoon cornstarch
- fresh cilantro leaves

Directions:

1. Make the marinade by combining the soy sauce, dry sherry, brown sugar, water, rice vinegar, garlic, ginger and crushed red pepper flakes. Pour the marinade over the chicken legs, cover and let the chicken marinate for 1 to 4 hours in the refrigerator.
2. Preheat the toaster oven to 380°F.
3. Transfer the chicken from the marinade to the air fryer oven, transferring any extra marinade to a small saucepan. Air-fry at 380°F for 8 minutes. Flip the chicken over and continue to air-fry for another 6 minutes, watching to make sure it doesn't brown too much.
4. While the chicken is cooking, bring the reserved marinade to a simmer on the stovetop. Dissolve the cornstarch in 2 tablespoons of water and stir this into the saucepan. Bring to a boil to thicken the sauce. Remove the garlic clove and slices of ginger from the sauce and set aside.
5. When the time is up on the air fryer oven, brush the thickened sauce on the chicken and air-fry for 3 more minutes. Remove the chicken from the air fryer oven and brush with the remaining sauce.
6. Serve over rice and sprinkle the cilantro leaves on top.

Sweet-and-sour Chicken

Servings: 6

Cooking Time: 10 Minutes

Ingredients:

- 1 cup pineapple juice
- 1 cup plus 3 tablespoons cornstarch, divided
- ¼ cup sugar
- ¼ cup ketchup
- ¼ cup apple cider vinegar
- 2 tablespoons soy sauce or tamari
- 1 teaspoon garlic powder, divided
- ¼ cup flour
- 1 tablespoon sesame seeds
- ½ teaspoon salt
- ¼ teaspoon ground black pepper
- 2 large eggs
- 2 pounds chicken breasts, cut into 1-inch cubes
- 1 red bell pepper, cut into 1-inch pieces
- 1 carrot, sliced into ¼-inch-thick rounds

Directions:

1. In a medium saucepan, whisk together the pineapple juice, 3 tablespoons of the cornstarch, the sugar, the ketchup, the apple cider vinegar, the soy sauce or tamari, and ½ teaspoon of the garlic powder. Cook over medium-low heat, whisking occasionally as the sauce thickens, about 6 minutes. Stir and set aside while preparing the chicken.
2. Preheat the toaster oven to 370°F.
3. In a medium bowl, place the remaining 1 cup of cornstarch, the flour, the sesame seeds, the salt, the remaining ½ teaspoon of garlic powder, and the pepper.
4. In a second medium bowl, whisk the eggs.
5. Working in batches, place the cubed chicken in the cornstarch mixture to lightly coat; then dip it into the egg mixture, and return it to the cornstarch mixture. Shake off the excess and place the coated chicken in the air fryer oven. Spray with cooking spray and air-fry for 5 minutes, and spray with more cooking spray. Cook an additional 3 to 5 minutes, or until completely cooked and golden brown.
6. On the last batch of chicken, add the bell pepper and carrot to the air fryer oven and cook with the chicken.
7. Place the cooked chicken and vegetables into a serving bowl and toss with the sweet-and-sour sauce to serve.

Italian Baked Chicken

Servings: 4

Cooking Time: 28 Minutes

Ingredients:

- 1 pound boneless, skinless chicken breasts
- ½ cup dry white wine
- 3 tablespoons olive oil
- 2 tablespoons white wine vinegar
- 2 tablespoons fresh lemon juice
- 2 teaspoons Italian seasoning
- 3 cloves garlic, minced
- ½ teaspoon kosher salt
- ¼ teaspoon freshly ground black pepper
- 4 slices salami, cut in half
- 3 tablespoons shredded Parmesan cheese

Directions:

1. If the chicken breasts are large and thick, slice each breast in half lengthwise. Place the chicken in a shallow baking dish.
2. Combine the white wine, olive oil, vinegar, lemon juice, Italian seasoning, garlic, salt, and pepper in a small bowl. Pour over the chicken breasts. Cover and refrigerate for 2 to 8 hours, turning the chicken occasionally to coat.
3. Preheat the toaster oven to 375 °F.
4. Drain the chicken, discarding the marinade, and place the chicken in an ungreased 12 x 12-inch baking pan. Bake, uncovered, for 20 to 25 minutes or until the chicken is done and a meat thermometer registers 165 °F. Place one slice salami (two pieces) on top of each piece of the chicken. Sprinkle the Parmesan evenly over the chicken breasts and broil for 2 to 3 minutes, or until the cheese is melted and starting to brown.

Chicken Breast With Chermoula Sauce

Servings: 4

Cooking Time: 15 Minutes

Ingredients:

- Chicken Ingredients
- 2 boneless skinless chicken breasts 1 tablespoon olive oil
- 1 teaspoon salt
- 1 teaspoon pepper
- Chermoula Ingredients
- 1 cup fresh cilantro
- 1 cup fresh parsley
- ¼ cup fresh mint
- ½ teaspoon red chili flakes
- ½ teaspoon cumin seeds
- ½ teaspoon coriander seeds
- 3 garlic cloves, peeled
- ½ cup extra virgin olive oil
- 1 lemon, zested and juiced
- ¾ teaspoons smoked paprika
- ¾ teaspoons salt

Directions:

1. Combine all the chermoula sauce ingredients in a blender or food processor. Pulse until smooth. Taste and add salt if needed. Place into a bowl and set aside.
2. Slice the chicken breast in half lengthwise and lightly pound with a meat tenderizer until both halves are about
3. ½-inch thick.
4. Preheat the toaster oven to 430°F.
5. Line the food tray with foil, then place the chicken breasts on the tray. Drizzle chicken with olive oil and season with salt and pepper.
6. Insert the food tray at top position in the preheated oven.
7. Select the Air Fry function, adjust time to 15 minutes, and press Start/Pause.
8. Remove when the chicken breast reaches an internal temperature of 160°F. Allow the chicken to rest for 5 minutes.
9. Brush the chermoula sauce over the chicken, or serve chicken with chermoula sauce on the side.

Quick Chicken For Filling

Servings: 2

Cooking Time: 8 Minutes

Ingredients:

- 1 pound chicken tenders, skinless and boneless
- ½ teaspoon ground cumin
- ½ teaspoon garlic powder
- cooking spray

Directions:

1. Sprinkle raw chicken tenders with seasonings.
2. Spray air fryer oven lightly with cooking spray to prevent sticking.
3. Place chicken in air fryer oven in single layer.
4. Air-fry at 390°F for 4 minutes, turn chicken strips over, and air-fry for an additional 4 minutes.
5. Test for doneness. Thick tenders may require an additional minute or two.

Chicken Nuggets

Servings: 20

Cooking Time: 14 Minutes

Ingredients:

- 1 pound boneless, skinless chicken thighs, cut into 1-inch chunks
- ¾ teaspoon salt
- ½ teaspoon black pepper
- ½ teaspoon garlic powder
- ½ teaspoon onion powder
- ½ cup flour
- 2 eggs, beaten
- ½ cup panko breadcrumbs
- 3 tablespoons plain breadcrumbs
- oil for misting or cooking spray

Directions:

1. In the bowl of a food processor, combine chicken, ½ teaspoon salt, pepper, garlic powder, and onion powder. Process in short pulses until chicken is very finely chopped and well blended.
2. Place flour in one shallow dish and beaten eggs in another. In a third dish or plastic bag, mix together the panko crumbs, plain breadcrumbs, and ¼ teaspoon salt.
3. Shape chicken mixture into small nuggets. Dip nuggets in flour, then eggs, then panko crumb mixture.
4. Spray nuggets on both sides with oil or cooking spray and place in air fryer oven in a single layer, close but not overlapping.
5. Air-fry at 360°F for 10 minutes. Spray with oil and cook 4 minutes, until chicken is done and coating is golden brown.
6. Repeat step 5 to cook remaining nuggets.

Italian Roasted Chicken Thighs

Servings: 6

Cooking Time: 14 Minutes

Ingredients:

- 6 boneless chicken thighs
- ½ teaspoon dried oregano
- ½ teaspoon garlic powder
- ½ teaspoon sea salt
- ½ teaspoon black pepper
- ¼ teaspoon crushed red pepper flakes

Directions:

1. Pat the chicken thighs with paper towel.
2. In a small bowl, mix the oregano, garlic powder, salt, pepper, and crushed red pepper flakes. Rub the spice mixture onto the chicken thighs.
3. Preheat the toaster oven to 400°F.
4. Place the chicken thighs in the air fryer oven and spray with cooking spray. Air-fry for 10 minutes, turn over, and cook another 4 minutes. When cooking completes, the internal temperature should read 165°F.

Curry Powder

Servings: 1

Cooking Time: 5 Minutes

Ingredients:

- ½ cup coriander seeds
- 2 tablespoons ground cumin
- 2 tablespoons black peppercorns
- 1 tablespoon sesame seeds
- 1 tablespoon cardamom seeds, extracted from the pods
- 2 small dried chili peppers
- 3 tablespoons turmeric
- 2 tablespoons ground ginger

Directions:

1. Combine the coriander seeds, cumin, peppercorns, sesame seeds, cardamom seeds, and chili peppers in an oiled or nonstick 8½ × 8½ × 2-inch square baking (cake) pan.
2. TOAST once, then turn with tongs and toast again, or continue toasting and turning until evenly toasted. Cool and grind the spices in a blender until the mixture becomes a powder. Add the turmeric and ground ginger and mix well. Store in a covered container in the refrigerator.

Pesto-crusted Chicken

Servings: 2

Cooking Time: 31 Minutes

Ingredients:

- Pesto:
- 1 cup fresh cilantro, parsley, and basil leaves
- 3 tablespoons nonfat plain yogurt
- ¼ cup pine nuts, walnut, or pecans
- 3 tablespoons grated Parmesan cheese
- 2 peeled garlic cloves
- 1 tablespoon lemon juice
- 3 tablespoons olive oil
- Salt and freshly ground black pepper to taste
- 2 skinless, boneless chicken breast halves

Directions:

1. Preheat the toaster oven to 450° F.
2. Blend the pesto ingredients in a blender or food processor until smooth. Set aside.
3. Place the chicken breast halves in an oiled or nonstick 8½ × 8½ × 2-inch square (cake) pan. With a butter knife or spatula, spread the mixture liberally on both sides of each chicken breast. Cover the dish with aluminum foil.
4. BAKE, covered, for 25 minutes, or until the chicken is tender. Remove from the oven and uncover.
5. BROIL for 6 minutes, or until the pesto coating is lightly browned.

Jerk Chicken Drumsticks

Servings: 2

Cooking Time: 20 Minutes

Ingredients:

- 1 or 2 cloves garlic
- 1 inch of fresh ginger
- 2 serrano peppers, (with seeds if you like it spicy, seeds removed for less heat)
- 1 teaspoon ground allspice
- 1 teaspoon ground nutmeg
- 1 teaspoon chili powder
- ½ teaspoon dried thyme
- ½ teaspoon ground cinnamon
- ½ teaspoon paprika
- 1 tablespoon brown sugar
- 1 teaspoon soy sauce
- 2 tablespoons vegetable oil
- 6 skinless chicken drumsticks

Directions:

1. Combine all the ingredients except the chicken in a small chopper or blender and blend to a paste. Make slashes into the meat of the chicken drumsticks and rub the spice blend all over the chicken (a pair of plastic gloves makes this really easy). Transfer the rubbed chicken to a non-reactive covered container and let the chicken marinate for at least 30 minutes or overnight in the refrigerator.
2. Preheat the toaster oven to 400°F.
3. Transfer the drumsticks to the air fryer oven. Air-fry for 10 minutes. Turn the drumsticks over and air-fry for another 10 minutes. Serve warm with some rice and vegetables or a green salad.

Coconut Chicken With Apricot-ginger Sauce

Servings: 4

Cooking Time: 8 Minutes

Ingredients:

- 1½ pounds boneless, skinless chicken tenders, cut in large chunks (about 1¼ inches)
- salt and pepper
- ½ cup cornstarch
- 2 eggs
- 1 tablespoon milk
- 3 cups shredded coconut (see below)
- oil for misting or cooking spray
- Apricot-Ginger Sauce
- ½ cup apricot preserves
- 2 tablespoons white vinegar
- ¼ teaspoon ground ginger
- ¼ teaspoon low-sodium soy sauce
- 2 teaspoons white or yellow onion, grated or finely minced

Directions:

1. Mix all ingredients for the Apricot-Ginger Sauce well and let sit for flavors to blend while you cook the chicken.
2. Season chicken chunks with salt and pepper to taste.
3. Place cornstarch in a shallow dish.
4. In another shallow dish, beat together eggs and milk.
5. Place coconut in a third shallow dish. (If also using panko breadcrumbs, as suggested below, stir them to mix well.)
6. Spray air fryer oven with oil or cooking spray.
7. Dip each chicken chunk into cornstarch, shake off excess, and dip in egg mixture.
8. Shake off excess egg mixture and roll lightly in coconut or coconut mixture. Spray with oil.
9. Place coated chicken chunks in air fryer oven in a single layer, close together but without sides touching.
10. Air-fry at 360˚F for 4 minutes, stop, and turn chunks over.
11. Cook an additional 4 minutes or until chicken is done inside and coating is crispy brown.
12. Repeat steps 9 through 11 to cook remaining chicken chunks.

Fried Chicken

Servings: 4

Cooking Time: 40 Minutes

Ingredients:

- 12 skin-on chicken drumsticks
- 1 cup buttermilk
- 1½ cups all-purpose flour
- 1 tablespoon smoked paprika
- ¾ teaspoon celery salt
- ¾ teaspoon dried mustard
- ½ teaspoon garlic powder
- ½ teaspoon freshly ground black pepper
- ½ teaspoon sea salt
- ½ teaspoon dried thyme
- ¼ teaspoon dried oregano
- 4 large eggs
- Oil spray (hand-pumped)

Directions:

1. Place the chicken and buttermilk in a medium bowl, cover, and refrigerate for at least 1 hour, up to overnight.
2. Preheat the toaster oven to 375°F on AIR FRY for 5 minutes.
3. In a large bowl, stir the flour, paprika, celery salt, mustard, garlic powder, pepper, salt, thyme, and oregano until well mixed.
4. Beat the eggs until frothy in a medium bowl and set them beside the flour.
5. Place the air-fryer basket in the baking tray and generously spray it with the oil.
6. Dredge a chicken drumstick in the flour, then the eggs, and then in the flour again, thickly coating it, and place the drumstick in the basket. Repeat with 5 more drumsticks and spray them all lightly with the oil on all sides.
7. In position 2, air fry for 20 minutes, turning halfway through, until golden brown and crispy with an internal temperature of 165°F.
8. Repeat with the remaining chicken, covering the cooked chicken loosely with foil to keep it warm. Serve.

Foiled Rosemary Chicken Breasts

Servings: 2

Cooking Time: 30 Minutes

Ingredients:

- 2 skinless, boneless chicken breast halves
- Sauce:
- 3 tablespoons dry white wine
- 1 tablespoon Dijon mustard
- 2 tablespoons nonfat plain yogurt
- Salt and freshly ground black pepper to taste
- 2 rosemary sprigs

Directions:

1. Preheat the toaster oven to 400° F.
2. Place each breast on a 12 × 12-inch square of heavy-duty aluminum foil (or regular foil doubled) and turn up the edges of the foil.
3. Mix together the sauce ingredients and spoon over the chicken breasts. Lay a rosemary sprig on each breast. Bring up the edges of the foil and fold to form a sealed packet.
4. BAKE for 25 minutes or until juices run clear when the meat is pierced with a fork. Remove the rosemary sprigs.
5. BROIL for 5 minutes, or until lightly browned. Replace the sprigs and serve.

VEGETABLES AND VEGETARIAN

Eggplant And Tomato Slices

Servings: 4

Cooking Time: 36 Minutes

Ingredients:

- 2 tablespoons olive oil
- ¼ teaspoon garlic powder
- 4½-inch-thick slices eggplant
- 4 ¼-inch-thick slices fresh tomato
- 2 tablespoons tomato sauce or salsa
- ½ cup shredded Parmesan cheese
- Salt and freshly ground black pepper to taste
- 2 tablespoons chopped fresh basil, cilantro, parsley, or oregano

Directions:

1. Whisk together the oil and garlic powder in a small bowl. Brush each eggplant slice with the mixture and place in an oiled or nonstick 8½ × 8½ × 2-inch square baking (cake) pan.
2. BROIL for 20 minutes. Remove the pan from the oven and turn the pieces with tongs. Top each with a slice of tomato and broil another 10 minutes, or until tender. Remove the pan from the oven, brush each slice with tomato sauce or salsa, and sprinkle generously with Parmesan cheese. Season to taste with salt and pepper. Broil again for 6 minutes, until the tops are browned.
3. Garnish with the fresh herb and serve.

Fingerling Potatoes

Servings: 4

Cooking Time: 15 Minutes

Ingredients:

- 1 pound fingerling potatoes
- 1 tablespoon light olive oil
- ½ teaspoon dried parsley
- ½ teaspoon lemon juice
- coarsely ground sea salt

Directions:

1. Cut potatoes in half lengthwise.
2. In a large bowl, combine potatoes, oil, parsley, and lemon juice. Stir well to coat potatoes.
3. Place potatoes in air fryer oven and air-fry at 360°F for 15 minutes or until lightly browned and tender inside.
4. Sprinkle with sea salt before serving.

Lentil-stuffed Zucchini

Servings: 2

Cooking Time: 50 Minutes

Ingredients:

- 2 large zucchini
- 2 teaspoons olive oil
- 1 (15-ounce) can low-sodium lentils, drained and rinsed
- 1 large tomato, chopped
- 1 scallion, both white and green parts, chopped
- ½ jalapeño pepper, minced
- ½ cup corn kernels, fresh or frozen (thawed)
- 1 tablespoon fresh cilantro, chopped
- 1 teaspoon minced garlic
- 1 teaspoon ground cumin
- ¼ teaspoon chili powder
- ½ cup shredded Monterey Jack cheese

Directions:

1. Preheat the toaster oven to 400°F on BAKE for 5 minutes.
2. Line the baking tray with parchment paper.
3. Cut the zucchini in half lengthwise and scoop out the insides so that you have a hollow shell (about ¼-inch thick all the way around).
4. Lightly oil both sides of the zucchini shells and set them on the baking sheet.
5. In a large bowl, stir the lentils, tomato, scallion, jalapeño, corn, cilantro, garlic, cumin, and chili powder until well mixed.
6. Spoon the lentil mixture into the zucchini and top with the cheese.
7. Bake for 50 minutes. The zucchini should be tender, the filling heated through, and the cheese melted and lightly browned. Serve.

Roasted Eggplant Halves With Herbed Ricotta

Servings: 3

Cooking Time: 20 Minutes

Ingredients:

- 3 5- to 6-ounce small eggplants, stemmed
- Olive oil spray
- ¼ teaspoon Table salt
- ¼ teaspoon Ground black pepper
- ½ cup Regular or low-fat ricotta
- 1½ tablespoons Minced fresh basil leaves
- 1¼ teaspoons Minced fresh oregano leaves
- Honey

Directions:

1. Preheat the toaster oven to 325°F (or 330°F, if that's the closest setting).
2. Cut the eggplants in half lengthwise. Set them cut side up on your work surface. Using the tip of a paring knife, make a series of slits about three-quarters down into the flesh of each eggplant half; work at a 45-degree angle to the (former) stem across the vegetable and make the slits about ½ inch apart. Make a second set of equidistant slits at a 90-degree angle to the first slits, thus creating a crosshatch pattern in the vegetable.
3. Generously coat the cut sides of the eggplants with olive oil spray. Sprinkle the salt and pepper over the cut surfaces.
4. Set the eggplant halves cut side up in the air fryer oven with as much air space between them as possible. Air-fry undisturbed for 20 minutes, or until soft and golden.
5. Use kitchen tongs to gently transfer the eggplant halves to serving plates or a platter. Cool for 5 minutes.
6. Whisk the ricotta, basil, and oregano in a small bowl until well combined. Top the eggplant halves with this mixture. Drizzle the halves with honey to taste before serving warm.

Roasted Ratatouille Vegetables

Servings: 15

Cooking Time: 2 Minutes

Ingredients:

- 1 baby or Japanese eggplant, cut into 1½-inch cubes
- 1 red pepper, cut into 1-inch chunks
- 1 yellow pepper, cut into 1-inch chunks
- 1 zucchini, cut into 1-inch chunks
- 1 clove garlic, minced
- ½ teaspoon dried basil
- 1 tablespoon olive oil
- salt and freshly ground black pepper
- ¼ cup sliced sun-dried tomatoes in oil
- 2 tablespoons chopped fresh basil

Directions:

1. Preheat the toaster oven to 400°F.
2. Toss the eggplant, peppers and zucchini with the garlic, dried basil, olive oil, salt and freshly ground black pepper.
3. Air-fry the vegetables at 400°F for 15 minutes.
4. As soon as the vegetables are tender, toss them with the sliced sun-dried tomatoes and fresh basil and serve.

Yogurt Zucchini With Onion

Servings: 4

Cooking Time: 30 Minutes

Ingredients:

- ½ cup plain fat-free yogurt
- 1 tablespoon unbleached flour
- 4 small zucchini, scrubbed and sliced into ½-inch strips
- 3 tablespoons minced fresh onion
- 1 tablespoon olive oil
- 3 tablespoons pine nuts, ground in a blender
- Salt and freshly ground black pepper

Directions:

1. Preheat the toaster oven to 400° F.
2. Whisk together the yogurt and flour in a small bowl until smooth. Transfer to a 1-quart 8½ × 8½ × 4-inch ovenproof baking dish. Add all the remaining ingredients, mixing well. Adjust the seasonings to taste. Cover the dish with aluminum foil.
3. BAKE, covered, for 25 minutes, or until the zucchini is tender. Uncover and toss gently to blend.
4. BROIL for 5 minutes, or until the top is lightly browned.

Stuffed Onions

Servings: 6

Cooking Time: 27 Minutes

Ingredients:

- 6 Small 3½- to 4-ounce yellow or white onions
- Olive oil spray
- 6 ounces Bulk sweet Italian sausage meat (gluten-free, if a concern)
- 9 Cherry tomatoes, chopped
- 3 tablespoons Seasoned Italian-style dried bread crumbs (gluten-free, if a concern)
- 3 tablespoons (about ½ ounce) Finely grated Parmesan cheese

Directions:

1. Preheat the toaster oven to 325°F (or 330°F, if that's the closest setting).
2. Cut just enough off the root ends of the onions so they will stand up on a cutting board when this end is turned down. Carefully peel off just the brown, papery skin. Now cut the top quarter off each and place the onion back on the cutting board with this end facing up. Use a flatware spoon (preferably a serrated grapefruit spoon) or a melon baller to scoop out the "insides" (interior layers) of the onion, leaving enough of the bottom and side walls so that the onion does not collapse. Depending on the thickness of the layers in the onion, this may be one or two of those layers—or even three, if they're very thin.
3. Coat the insides and outsides of the onions with olive oil spray. Set the onion "shells" in the air fryer oven and air-fry for 15 minutes.
4. Meanwhile, make the filling. Set a medium skillet over medium heat for a couple of minutes, then crumble in the sausage meat. Cook, stirring often, until browned, about 4 minutes. Transfer the contents of the skillet to a medium bowl (leave the fat behind in the skillet or add it to the bowl, depending on your cross-trainer regimen). Stir in the tomatoes, bread crumbs, and cheese until well combined.
5. When the onions are ready, use a nonstick-safe spatula to gently transfer them to a cutting board. Increase the air fryer oven's temperature to 350°F .
6. Pack the sausage mixture into the onion shells, gently compacting the filling and mounding it up at the top.
7. When the machine is at temperature, set the onions stuffing side up in the air fryer oven with at least ¼ inch between them. Air-fry for 12 minutes, or until lightly browned and sizzling hot.
8. Use a nonstick-safe spatula, and perhaps a flatware fork for balance, to transfer the onions to a cutting board or serving platter. Cool for 5 minutes before serving.

Roasted Fennel Salad

Servings: 3

Cooking Time: 20 Minutes

Ingredients:

- 3 cups (about ¾ pound) Trimmed fennel, roughly chopped
- 1½ tablespoons Olive oil
- ¼ teaspoon Table salt
- ¼ teaspoon Ground black pepper
- 1½ tablespoons White balsamic vinegar

Directions:

1. Preheat the toaster oven to 400°F.
2. Toss the fennel, olive oil, salt, and pepper in a large bowl until the fennel is well coated in the oil.
3. When the machine is at temperature, pour the fennel into the air fryer oven, spreading it out into as close to one layer as possible. Air-fry for 20 minutes, tossing and rearranging the fennel pieces twice so that any covered or touching parts get exposed to the air currents, until golden at the edges and softened.
4. Pour the fennel into a serving bowl. Add the vinegar while hot. Toss well, then cool a couple of minutes before serving. Or serve at room temperature.

Fried Corn On The Cob

Servings: 2

Cooking Time: 10 Minutes

Ingredients:

- 1½ tablespoons Regular or low-fat mayonnaise (not fat-free; gluten-free, if a concern)
- 1½ teaspoons Minced garlic
- ¼ teaspoon Table salt
- ¾ cup Plain panko bread crumbs (gluten-free, if a concern)
- 3 4-inch lengths husked and de-silked corn on the cob
- Vegetable oil spray

Directions:

1. Preheat the toaster oven to 400°F.
2. Stir the mayonnaise, garlic, and salt in a small bowl until well combined. Spread the panko on a dinner plate.
3. Brush the mayonnaise mixture over the kernels of a piece of corn on the cob. Set the corn in the bread crumbs, then roll, pressing gently, to coat it. Lightly coat with vegetable oil spray. Set it aside, then coat the remaining piece(s) of corn in the same way.
4. Set the coated corn on the cob in the air fryer oven with as much air space between the pieces as possible. Air-fry undisturbed for 10 minutes, or until brown and crisp along the coating.
5. Use kitchen tongs to gently transfer the pieces of corn to a wire rack. Cool for 5 minutes before serving.

Classic Baked Potatoes

Servings: 4

Cooking Time: 50 Minutes

Ingredients:

- 4 medium baking potatoes,
- scrubbed and pierced with a fork

Directions:

1. Preheat the toaster oven to 450° F.
2. BAKE the potatoes on the oven rack for 50 minutes, or until tender when pierced with a fork.

Rosemary Roasted Potatoes With Lemon

Servings: 12

Cooking Time: 4 Minutes

Ingredients:

- 1 pound small red-skinned potatoes, halved or cut into bite-sized chunks
- 1 tablespoon olive oil
- 1 teaspoon finely chopped fresh rosemary
- ¼ teaspoon salt
- freshly ground black pepper
- 1 tablespoon lemon zest

Directions:

1. Preheat the toaster oven to 400°F.
2. Toss the potatoes with the olive oil, rosemary, salt and freshly ground black pepper.
3. Air-fry for 12 minutes (depending on the size of the chunks), tossing the potatoes a few times throughout the cooking process.
4. As soon as the potatoes are tender to a knifepoint, toss them with the lemon zest and more salt if desired.

Crisp Cajun Potato Wedges

Servings: 2

Cooking Time: 70 Minutes

Ingredients:

- 2 medium baking potatoes, scrubbed, halved, and cut lengthwise into ½-inch-wide wedges
- 1 tablespoon vegetable oil
- Cajun seasonings:
- ¼ teaspoon chili powder
- ⅛ teaspoon cayenne
- ⅛ teaspoon dry mustard
- ⅛ teaspoon salt
- ⅛ teaspoon cumin
- ¼ teaspoon onion powder
- ¼ teaspoon paprika

Directions:

1. Preheat the toaster oven to 450° F.
2. Soak the potato wedges in cold water for 10 minutes to crisp. Drain on paper towels. Brush with the oil.
3. Combine the Cajun seasonings in a small bowl, add the wedges, and toss to coat well. Transfer to an oiled or nonstick 8½ × 8½ × 2-inch square baking (cake) pan.
4. BAKE, covered, for 40 minutes, or until the potatoes are tender. Carefully remove the cover.
5. BROIL for 20 minutes to crisp, turning with a tongs every 5 minutes until the desired crispness is achieved.

Potato Skins

Servings: 4

Cooking Time: 20 Minutes

Ingredients:

- 4 potato shells

Directions:

1. Place 4 potato shells in an oiled or nonstick 8½ × 8½ × 2-inch square baking (cake) pan.
2. Brush, sprinkle, and fill with a variety of seasonings or ingredients.
3. BROIL 20 minutes, or until browned and crisped to your preference.

DESSERTS

Apricot Coffee Cake

Servings: 1

Cooking Time: 15 Minutes

Ingredients:

- 2 cups baking mix
- 3 ounces cream cheese
- ¼ cup unsalted butter
- ½ cup chopped pecans, toasted
- ⅓ cup whole milk
- ¾ cup apricot preserves
- GLAZE
- 1 cup confectioners' sugar
- ¼ teaspoon almond extract
- 1 to 2 tablespoons whole milk

Directions:

1. Preheat the toaster oven to 425 °F. Grease a 12 x 12-inch baking pan.
2. Place the baking mix in a large bowl. Using a pastry cutter or two knives, cut the cream cheese and butter into the baking mix until the mixture is crumbly throughout. Add the pecans and milk and mix well.
3. Turn the dough onto a lightly floured surface and knead lightly about 8 times. Roll the dough into a 12 x 8-inch rectangle. Place the rolled dough diagonally on the prepared pan. Spread the preserves lengthwise down the center of the dough. Make 2 ½-inch cuts at 1-inch intervals on both sides of the filling. Fold the strips over the preserves, overlapping in the center. Bake for 15 minutes or until golden brown.
4. Make the Glaze: Whisk the confectioners' sugar, almond extract, and 1 tablespoon milk in a small bowl until smooth. Add additional milk, as needed, to make a glaze consistency.
5. Drizzle the glaze over the warm coffee cake.

Mississippi Mud Brownies

Servings: 16

Cooking Time: 34 Minutes

Ingredients:

- Nonstick cooking spray
- 3 tablespoons unsweetened cocoa powder
- ¼ cup canola or vegetable oil
- ¼ cup unsalted butter, softened
- 1 cup granulated sugar
- 2 large eggs
- 1 teaspoon pure vanilla extract
- ¾ cup all-purpose flour
- ½ teaspoon table salt
- ½ cup pecan pieces, toasted
- 2 cups mini marshmallows
- FROSTING
- ¼ cup unsalted butter, melted
- 3 tablespoons unsweetened cocoa powder
- ½ teaspoon pure vanilla extract
- 2 cups confectioners' sugar
- 2 to 3 tablespoons whole milk

Directions:

1. Preheat the toaster oven to 350°F. Spray an 8-inch square baking pan with nonstick cooking spray.
2. Beat the cocoa and oil in a large bowl with a handheld mixer at medium speed. Add the butter and mix until smooth. Beat in the granulated sugar. Add the eggs, one at a time, mixing after each addition. Add the vanilla and mix. On low speed, blend in the flour and salt. Stir in the pecans.
3. Pour the batter into the prepared pan. Bake for 28 to 32 minutes, or until a wooden pick inserted into the center comes out clean.
4. Remove the brownies from the oven and sprinkle the marshmallows over the top. Return to the oven and bake for about 2 minutes or until the marshmallows are puffed. Place on a wire rack and let cool completely.
5. Meanwhile, make the frosting: Combine the butter, cocoa, vanilla, confectioners' sugar, and 2 tablespoons milk in a large bowl. Beat until smooth. If needed for the desired consistency, add additional milk. Frost the cooled brownies.

Soft Peanut Butter Cookies

Servings: 12

Cooking Time: 20 Minutes

Ingredients:

- 1/2 cup vegetable shortening
- 1/2 cup peanut butter
- 1 1/4 cups light brown sugar
- 1 egg
- 1 teaspoon vanilla
- 1/2 teaspoon salt
- 1 1/2 cups flour
- 1 teaspoon baking soda
- Sugar crystals

Directions:

1. Preheat the toaster oven to 275°F.
2. Using the flat beater attachment, beat shortening, peanut butter, brown sugar, egg, and vanilla at a medium setting until well blended.
3. Reduce speed to low and gradually add dry ingredients until blended. Dough will be crumbly.
4. Roll 3 tablespoon-size portions of the dough into a ball. Place on ungreased cookie sheet.
5. Press to 1/2-inch thick. Sprinkle with sugar crystals.
6. Bake 18 to 20 minutes. Do not overcook.

Fried Snickers Bars

Servings: 8

Cooking Time: 4 Minutes

Ingredients:

- ⅓ cup All-purpose flour
- 1 Large egg white(s), beaten until foamy
- 1½ cups (6 ounces) Vanilla wafer cookie crumbs
- 8 Fun-size (0.6-ounce/17-gram) Snickers bars, frozen
- Vegetable oil spray

Directions:

1. Preheat the toaster oven to 400°F.
2. Set up and fill three shallow soup plates or small pie plates on your counter: one for the flour, one for the beaten egg white(s), and one for the cookie crumbs.
3. Unwrap the frozen candy bars. Dip one in the flour, turning it to coat on all sides. Gently stir any excess, then set it in the beaten egg white(s). Turn it to coat all sides, even the ends, then let any excess egg white slip back into the rest. Set the candy bar in the cookie crumbs. Turn to coat on all sides, even the ends. Dip the candy bar back in the egg white(s) a second time, then into the cookie crumbs a second time, making sure you have an even coating all around. Coat the covered candy bar all over with vegetable oil spray. Set aside so you can dip and coat the remaining candy bars.
4. Set the coated candy bars in the pan with as much air space between them as possible. Air-fry undisturbed for 4 minutes, or until golden brown.
5. Remove the pan from the machine and let the candy bars cool in the pan for 10 minutes. Use a nonstick-safe spatula to transfer them to a wire rack and cool for 5 minutes more before chowing down.

Keto Cheesecake Cups

Servings: 6

Cooking Time: 10 Minutes

Ingredients:

- 8 ounces cream cheese
- ¼ cup plain whole-milk Greek yogurt
- 1 large egg
- 1 teaspoon pure vanilla extract
- 3 tablespoons monk fruit sweetener
- ¼ teaspoon salt
- ½ cup walnuts, roughly chopped

Directions:

1. Preheat the toaster oven to 315°F.
2. In a large bowl, use a hand mixer to beat the cream cheese together with the yogurt, egg, vanilla, sweetener, and salt. When combined, fold in the chopped walnuts.
3. Set 6 silicone muffin liners inside an air-fryer-safe pan.
4. Evenly fill the cupcake liners with cheesecake batter.
5. Carefully place the pan into the air fryer oven and air-fry for about 10 minutes, or until the tops are lightly browned and firm.
6. Carefully remove the pan when done and place in the refrigerator for 3 hours to firm up before serving.

Orange-glazed Brownies

Servings: 12

Cooking Time: 30 Minutes

Ingredients:

- 3 squares unsweetened chocolate
- 3 tablespoons margarine
- 1 cup sugar
- ½ cup orange juice
- 2 eggs
- 1½ cups unbleached flour
- 1 teaspoon baking powder
- Salt to taste
- 1 tablespoon grated orange zest
- Orange Glaze (recipe follows)

Directions:

1. BROIL the chocolate and margarine in an oiled or nonstick 8½ × 8½ × 2-inch square baking (cake) pan for 3 minutes, or until almost melted. Remove from the oven and stir until completely melted. Transfer the chocolate/margarine mixture to a medium bowl.
2. Beat in the sugar, orange juice, and eggs with an electric mixer. Stir in the flour, baking powder, salt, and orange zest and mix until well blended. Pour into the oiled or nonstick square cake pan.
3. BAKE at 350° F. for 30 minutes, or until a toothpick inserted in the center comes out clean. Make holes over the entire top by piercing with a fork or toothpick. Paint with Orange Glaze and cut into squares.

Orange Strawberry Flan

Servings: 4

Cooking Time: 45 Minutes

Ingredients:

- ¼ cup sugar
- ½ cup concentrated orange juice
- 1 12-ounce can low-fat evaporated milk
- 3 egg yolks
- 1 cup frozen strawberries, thawed and sliced, or 1 cup fresh strawberries, washed, stemmed, and sliced
- 4 fresh mint sprigs

Directions:

1. Preheat the toaster oven to 375° F.
2. Place the sugar in a baking pan and broil for 4 minutes, or until the sugar melts. Remove from the oven, stir briefly, and pour equal portions of the caramelized sugar into four 1-cup-size ovenproof dishes. Set aside.
3. Blend the orange juice, evaporated milk, and egg yolks in a food processor or blender until smooth. Transfer the mixture to a medium bowl and fold in the sliced strawberries. Pour the mixture in equal portions into the four dishes.
4. BAKE for 45 minutes, or until a knife inserted in the center comes out clean. Chill for several hours. The flan may be loosened by running a knife around the edge and inverted on individual plates or served in the dishes. Garnish with fresh mint sprigs.

Freezer-to-oven Chocolate Chip Cookies

Servings: 6

Cooking Time: 15 Minutes

Ingredients:

- 2 ½ cups all-purpose flour
- 1 teaspoon baking soda
- ½ teaspoon table salt
- ¼ teaspoon baking powder
- 1 cup unsalted butter, softened
- 1 cup packed dark brown sugar
- ¾ cup granulated sugar
- 2 large eggs
- 2 teaspoons pure vanilla extract
- 1 (12-ounce) package semisweet chocolate chips

Directions:

1. Preheat the toaster oven to 375°F. Line a 12 x 12-inch baking sheet with parchment paper.
2. Whisk the flour, baking soda, salt, and baking powder in a medium bowl; set aside.
3. Beat the butter, brown sugar, and granulated sugar in a large bowl with a handheld mixer at medium-high speed for 2 minutes or until creamy. Beat in the eggs, one at a time, beating well after each addition. Beat in the vanilla. Mix in the dry ingredients until blended. Stir in the chocolate chips.
4. Using a 2-tablespoon scoop, shape the batter into balls about 1 ½ inches in diameter. Arrange the cookies 1 inch apart on the prepared baking sheet. Bake for 13 to 15 minutes or until golden brown. Remove from the oven and let cool for 1 minute, then transfer the cookies to a wire rack.

Maple-glazed Pumpkin Pie

Servings: 2

Cooking Time: 10 Minutes

Ingredients:

- Filling:
- 1 15-ounce can pumpkin pie filling
- 1 12-ounce can low-fat evaporated milk
- 1 egg
- 3 tablespoons maple syrup
- ½ teaspoon grated nutmeg
- ½ teaspoon ground ginger
- 1 teaspoon ground cinnamon
- Salt to taste
- 1 Apple Juice Piecrust, baked (recipe follows)
- Dark glaze:
- 3 tablespoons maple syrup
- 2 tablespoons dark brown sugar

Directions:

1. Preheat the toaster oven to 400° F.
2. Combine all the filling ingredients in a large bowl and beat with an electric mixer until smooth. Pour into the piecrust shell.
3. BAKE for 40 minutes, or until a knife inserted in the center comes out clean.
4. Combine the dark glaze ingredients in a baking pan.
5. BROIL for 5 minutes, or until bubbling. Remove from the oven and stir to dissolve the sugar. Broil again for 3 minutes, or until the liquid is thickened and the sugar is dissolved. Spoon on top of the cooled pumpkin pie, spreading evenly, then chill for at least 1 hour before serving.

CPSIA information can be obtained
at www.ICGtesting.com
Printed in the USA
BVHW050855040122
625439BV00013B/448